Semibreve

John F. Deane was born on Achill Island in 1943. He founded Poetry Ireland – the National Poetry Society – and *The Poetry Ireland Review* in 1978, and is the founder of The Dedalus Press, of which he was editor from 1985 until 2006. In 2008 he was visiting scholar in the Burns Library of Boston College. John F. Deane's poetry has been translated and published in France, Bulgaria, Macedonia, Romania, Italy, Slovakia, Sweden and other countries. His poems in Italian won the 2002 Premio Internazionale di Poesia Città di Marineo. His fiction has been published by Blackstaff Press in Belfast; his most recent novel *Where No Storms Come* was published by Blackstaff in 2011. He is the recipient of the O'Shaughnessy Award for Irish Poetry and the Marten Toonder Award for Literature. John F. Deane is a member of Aosdána, the body established by the Arts Council to honour artists 'whose work has made an outstanding contribution to the arts in Ireland'. His poetry has been shortlisted for the *Irish Times* Poetry Now Award and the T.S. Eliot Prize. In 2007 he was made Chevalier en l'ordre des arts et des lettres by the French government. In October 2011 Deane was awarded the Serbian prize the Golden Key of Smederevo, as well as the Laudomia Bonanni prize from L'Aquila, Italy.

Also by John F. Deane from Carcanet Press

Eye of the Hare
A Little Book of Hours
The Instruments of Art
Manhandling the Deity
Toccata and Fugue
Snow Falling on Chestnut Hill: New and Selected Poems

JOHN F. DEANE

Semibreve

CARCANET

First published in Great Britain in 2015 by
Carcanet Press Limited
Alliance House
Cross Street
Manchester M2 7AQ

www.carcanet.co.uk

We welcome your comments on our publications
Write to us at info@carcanet.co.uk

A CIP catalogue record for this book is available from the British Library

ISBN 978 1 84777 269 5

The publisher acknowledges financial assistance from Arts Council England

Typeset by XL Publishing Services, Exmouth
Printed and bound in England by SRP Ltd, Exeter

Acknowledgements

Agenda Magazine; *Bliza* (Poland); *Boulevard Magenta Magazine*; *Clifden 35: The Clifden Anthology 2012* (ed. Brendan Flynn); *The Christian Century* (USA); *The Furrow*; *Image* (USA); *Irish Times*; *PN Review*; *Poetry International Web*; *Poetry Review*; *Riddle Fence* (Canada); *Shine On Anthology* (Dedalus Press); *The SHOp*; *Stony Thursday Book* (ed. Paddy Bushe); *Sunday Miscellany*, RTE Radio; *The Tablet*; *Temenos*; *Visions International* (USA); *Warwick Review*; *The Works of Love* (Columba Press, 2010); *The Yellow Nib*; a selection of poems was published on the website www.molossus.co (ed. Sudeep Sen); 'Night Prayer' was written to a commission from the National Gallery of Ireland and published in *Lines of Vision* (Thames & Hudson, 2014); 'Museum of Country Life' was published in the anthology *What We Found There* (Dedalus Press, ed. Theo Dorgan). The sequence 'Blessed and Broken' is dedicated to Brendan McConvery C.Ss.R.

Contents

I

II

III

IV

I

Semibreve

I sat, in the island chapel, moor's edge, winter;
winds groaned and chistled round the walls outside,
the timbers creaked in the afterwarmth,

ghosts from the quenching slipped up through the rafters;
there was a souring emptiness though I sat entranced
by sacrament and my own minuscule being – when the walls

whispered – *Listen!* There was no-one. There was nothing.
Even the winds had died. And the chill winterlight
had dimmed. But a tiny chime had happened, vibrated

on my inner listening. The tiniest hint of spittle
tipped against my brow but there was nothing when I wiped
my hand across it. The door moaned again, a sudden breeze

forcing it and I stood, watchful, and shaken. That
was the first semibreve sounded of a gifted music.
I am day and night now, listening. Tuned for it, and waiting.

Viola d'Amore

I had been playing Bach on the great organ –
'A mighty fortress is our God' –
the church below me empty in the nowhere afternoon,
bombarde, clarion, celeste

and when I lifted fingers from the keys
it was, for a moment, eternity, and the walls of the world
contained nothing but the lingering breadth of the harmony,

rafters of the loft had lifted while the whole sky
trembled in a breeze that rippled slow across it
till all I knew was the touch of the fingers of Jesus

soft on my fingertips, my body
consciously drawing breath, my bones
refusing their earthy weight, and my soul
ringing with immortality.

Black and White

A hush will settle in about you, even in the ruck
    of crowds and traffic, an expectation
building (from within, without) and the words
    like a flock of redwing in the winter scutch-grass
shifting to be noised up into movement, some
ghosting memory, some vivifying stone
    or rainfall, finger-touch or weeping to take
the long-forgotten back into treasury: like the Mercy
    sister, in constraining black and white, who comes scarily
in through the music-room door, shoes knocking a hard
    rhythm on the wooden floor, books of scales and finger-exercises
tight against the starched guimpe over her breasts
as if Bach could never rise like larks out of the white
    notes, or Palestrina break in surf out of the black.

The Living-Room

for Raymond Deane

We worked to learn the notes, the sharps, the flats,
we tried the underlying harmonies;
remember how the piano pedal stuck?
and favourite drawing-room pieces (*The Robin's*

Return, The Maiden's Prayer) became such mush,
like re-rolled plasticine. There was that sheen on the grand
mahogany table, how our lemonade glasses
left rings that would not come off and oh! the blame!

Remember how we hid, watching the adults play
their money-games, how an inner light from the whiskey
glimmered, and firelight sent sparkles gambolling
from glass decanters on the sideboard? How perfect

in memory it all was. On the parlour floor, remember?
just there, before the hearth, the river-otter pelt, sleek
golden fur through the underhair, silk-feel and death-grin,
how it brought into the room the stealth of water-dog,

high-jinks and romping, teeth sunk in trout-flesh,
secrecy of den and holt, the chill, the sliming... We
held to the basics, arpeggios, chords and scales;
you mastered them, remember? They have eluded me.

Playing on the White Notes

For days now, white butterflies are a storm
low over the meadow; they come to rest awhile
on the white clover, their wings, for a moment, folded;

the early purity of the lambs is a little sullied
while over against the fence line, Michaelmas daisies
are gathering to themselves the light of the sun,

hoarding the white heat of summer to their roots
as if the autumn colourings, waiting in the wings,
might be absorbed into the slow white dirge

the winter plays, when the black of night
will take its loveliness only from the white
splintering of stars, white fullness of the moon.

Tuning

He was up in the choir-loft, tuning the pipes
of the old century's wind-pump organ; I heard
taps and bangs on metal, strange half-throated off-
notes, near-notes, puffs, sighs and cough-blasts;

and then he was playing – Bach, Buxtehude, Peters –
it was a young Jehovah's making, a bright hands-full
soaring over oceans of soul-light, filling the chill of the chapel
with a lush of breathing. Now, in my everyday listening,

for the poem, the music, I am Mary before the ash-soft fall
of the messenger, I am John after the disappearance
beyond the clouds; I listen to the silence beyond the thuck
and thudding of a day's importance, to hear the hum that figures

a countryside of darkness, the sounds of April
whispering over into May, the thunder of apple blossoms
dropping from the tree; I listen for the tune that my days make
in the works of love, in the notes' approximations to a symphony.

Theme and Variations

I

A fledgling goldfinch – that furze-blossom light
on the wings, that blood-cherry blush on the face –
lay on the driveway in its char of death; worms

had devoured the eyes, a hole in its breast
was lidded with flies, and all the help I could offer
was to lay it in grass under the dogwood hedge;

II

on the road a badger, overrun in the night,
lay tossed in dust, our brock, our secretive

low-tangled grey-within-grey and black-white
prowler, in a wet mess of itself; our hearts

III

are not of lead nor our bone-built scaffolding
of steel rods. Evening sunlight came shining clear

through the stained windows where we knelt

in penitential exercise; above us the saints in glory,
the angel tiers, the Christ enthroned, and over all

IV

the radiant spirit-dove; emeralds, scarlets,
the lapis lazuli, the gold, the story held
in bright magnificence. Gradually, in the light's

failing, the windows dulled, silver to grey-within-grey

then black, till all stood pale like photographic
negatives, the artistry still there, though as if
much more than light had abandoned it. Night

V

came dark; I stood by the Atlantic breakers, saw
the grey glint of the waves, all else vastness,

the breadth of the unknown; like tides the world

gives, and takes, but the spirit – willing order – holds
through the captivating watches of the night. Today

VI

there is late spring chaos across the valley,
reed-music of the wind sounds its three
sorrow-songs through the famine-abandoned village;

sheep browse on the high slopes, the skylark
lifts from heather tufts in a sustained
generosity of song, while over all the cuckoo,

back from its winter absence, calls out
the names of its countless generations
and a soft rain falls. I sit alone, listening;

VII

Andras Schiff on the car radio plays the Goldberg
Variations, the music of stream and steeple

strung in arithmetical certainties, the spirit's dance –
of Saraband, of Passepieds and Passacaglia –

keeping the day, the hope, the modulations
in the heart's control and the spirit holding

through the slow counterpoint and the unravelling.

Pipe Organ

From the organ console, the mirror
showed the empty church below, and my face
animated; I played, for myself alone,
Gelobet seist du, Jesu Christ,

and moved with some élan over manuals and pedalboard,
my body given over to a dance of faith: viol
da gamba – trembling strings, bourdon – the breathfulness
of the flute; and for a time

I was angel-messenger, heisted up between
green marble floor and cobalt sky, revelling
in Godness and the surgent
confidence of the organ.

★

When I climbed down
from the upper reaches of myself,
when the slow Amen had trailed
its silken skirts away across the sanctuary,

I crept in behind the organ
to revel once again in dust and rust and dowels,
in cobwebs on the unadorned
vertebrae of the pipes; brought back to worm-holed boards

radiant in reflected colours off the rose window
with tales of the one Source, the walking-on-red-dust roads
of the Christ, of the Love-dancer
whom the whole globe of earth could not enclose.

II

Great Northern Diver

Sometimes the sea, surging
through its seasonal gradations, comes

crashing in across the rocks and pier beyond Rusheen;
on Croaghaun the corrie brims,

dark water spilling over, gathering
a rust-brown iron and coursing down to ocean.

She who stands, each day, near dawn
to watch the morning bus out of Dooagh

leave for fresh-turned fields, stares vacantly out
over Atlantic waves that flick, sometimes, a salt spittle

against her face. She heard, last night,
the great northern diver far out, in the dark, offshore,

its long and withering cries, and she knows –
after the headlight beams of the bus have passed

on over the road and up the hill –
the rooster (cockerel, chanticleer, and cock-a-doodle-doo)

will be there, hoop-la, on the graveyard wall
crowing his name out in a flustering of wattles, earlobes, crest.

Soon she will turn, to go indoors, wondering
if ever there is a time we are other than alone.

Nora

The child stood, arms held wide,
grandmother unwinding skeins of wool from round his wrists

into a ball; she was teaching him
Jesus, who put the world together again: *all the king's horses...*

He fidgeted, while the breeze outside
stirred the pines to whispering; from the monastery tower the bell

told its three-times-three and then its nine
insistent messages, how the young girl prayed, engrossed with love.

Later, he would pick at the fraying jumper,
unravelling it, abstracted, thread by thread, 'wool-gathering again'

she scolded him. He saw her,
gravity's daughter, age weighing heavily on her;

she dressed in woollen black when her lover died
and he watched her guard the hearth and sigh like settling embers,

deft still with tongs, with poker and the toasting-fork;
he hurts still, remembering her, the threads irreparably broken.

Hydrangeas

Those late afternoons
when he had not come, she held grief

hard against her breasts,
knowing that living happens in the moments

between one dread
and another; like a dirge building between

one struck chord
and another. She would gather

lace-caps, forget-me-not blue,
with lilac highlights and a white trim, as if

in the heart of the hydrangea bush
she might find a stylite quiet, sand, considerate

scorpions and at least a scent
of honey; and she shaped a large bouquet

that would gather dust-talc
and the husks of flies and placed it

in a cut-glass vase
big before his early-morning mirror.

High Tide

Dust on the beads on the vanished woman's dressing-table,
a few grey hairs in the bristles of her brush,

a missal fat with cards in memory... I gazed
into her amber-surround small hand-mirror, as if one might expect

the long years watching would have left some trace, her eyes
looking back at me with some sign of love;

grief thickens with its selfishness, loss
to the ongrowing ego, though the vanished soul, we may believe,

is settling to the banquet of the blessed. From her front window
I see the waters of Blacksod Bay, down

over the famished fields, the fuchsia hedges, the bogland wastes;
somewhere a dog is barking, and an ass

brays loudly. Around the pier, I know, thick clumps of seaweed
sway and slap in ongoing process, tides

will leave them flopped and slithery for a few hours, then touch
their edges again to a salt wakefulness. She

processed her beads with a fulsome regularity, I could hear the sibilance
of her almost-silent prayers, that irritating

constancy. And what can we do with loss? Replace the mirror, draw
the curtains against the window, turn and go out.

Dolores

We mocked her, for her withered hand,
her side-legging walk, hare-lip, her stammering;

we were, all of us, guilty, and knew it; save when
after Mass, she opened shop and we came seeking

thruppence-worth, or sixpence, or a penny –
fruit pastilles and hard-gums, lucky-bags and liquorice pipes –

then was she mistress, for the nonce,
of weights and measures, of paper bags and paper pokes,

playing her jingle-jangle till-music; woman
with a preference for dusklight, who would have danced

on this one earth, under bright chandeliers
but held desire fast in old account-books with mouse-gnawed covers;

there is no geography to clarify such a life
from the wail out of the cramped womb to the silence; and what

do the scriptures say of life's banquet?
each guest and place at table, each minion, each bitter wine.

Dancing the Dance

I feared the craziness in her. She walked
always with determination, certain

of her direction. Then stopped, gazed round
as if some darkness had overwhelmed her. Or was it

light? She turned, and headed home. Her clothes
heavy and black, perpetual winter, perpetual

mourning, a black beret perched anxiously on sparse
grey hair. She lit candles in the parish church,

knelt a long time in almost stillness. For what
was it she knew, what was it touched her that had never

glanced against me? She danced sometimes in the rain, a slow
waltzing movement, her hands embracing air. Years

later, long after she disappeared and her house collapsed
in lethargy, she is a beacon for my own, resisting, faith.

Midwife

Now all the beech, in copse and hedgerow,
stand in saffron evening-gowns; against the long black nights

memories hull like leaves
blown into garden-corners. Ivy has darkened the windows

of Mamie's house, chaffinches linger in the branches of the thorn
and rain falls through missing slates of the low roof.

There is a task given to us, and to every task a season – so
when the back wall of her drawing-room

gave birth to a green-brown stain
shaped like the rampant bull of Lascaux caves, she moved

the delicate furnishings out and closed the door.
Mamie. Mid-wife. Perpetually on call. She could handle

the elemental cells, but for her the long road home
was on rutted surfaces, sycamores and poplars

darkening every turn; the breeze sent shuffle-noises through the trees,
no-one was there, nor anything to hold to. So

she stitched her days together with cigarettes, the chill nights
with the bitterness of gin; she left

warmth of her fingers on the flesh of generations
and left her cold body

draped across stained arms of the sofa, while rodents gnawed
the leathern turns of her heels.

Blueberries

I am in California. The moon —
colour of grandmother's Irish butter — is lifting

over the Mount Diablo hills and the sky
is tinged a ripening strawberry. You sleep

thousands of miles from me and I pray your dreams
are a tranquil sea. Eight hours back

you watched this moon, our love-, our marriage-moon,
rise silently over our Dublin suburb, and you

phoned to tell me of it. I sit in stillness
though I am called where death is by; I am eating

night and grief in the sweet-bitter flesh
of blueberries, coating tongue and lips with juice

that this my kiss across unconscionable distances
touch to your lips with the fullness of our loving.

Egg-Woman

She was widowed, young; three sons,
leaving her, gradually: for Coventry, Glasgow, Liverpool. She lived

tending graves; beating away
importunate ghosts. Sitting alone she whimpered sometimes,

like a favoured animal
kept outside in the rains. It was a long life, unaltering; perhaps

altering more than that.
Mouse-eared chickweed in the interstices of the shed, ebullient

rosebay willowherb
in the graveyard. She knew the every-morning miracle of brown eggs

stamped with a small bronze feather,
the every-evening watchfulness of the red-gold vixen, of the slattern
                                                                    harrier

hovering over the scattered fluff-balls
of fattening chicks. To be woman, mother, alone again

to sit by a chivvying fire
under the fading reproduction of Mary-in-Blue who was holding close

her golden son. She walked
the hesitant moist corridors between the graves, listening out for

greetings from her gravid neighbours
who used to walk with her on fair days and bonfire nights

to a celebration of the gift of flames.
Now she was nursing silence to her breasts, its threat, its intimacy.

III

The Workhouse

Two Boys

They are playing hide-and-seek among rocks;
you can hear their laughter, their voices rising in dispute,

sinking again to whispers;
Yeshua, Yohanan, cousins,

different time and language, same
body-shapes, same dreams –

where the adults speak of Elohim, of Yahweh.
In the west of Ireland, same

gestures, different language, two boys, brothers,
dusk and the murmuring of rosary;

slow years of ease and innocence,
little knowing how living will ground itself,

how the winter fuchsia is cut to stump
and waits, as if in death,

how the juniper berry
swells to blue, a beauty shot with bitterness;

child, on the red shaft of a cart:
child, on the hard rump of a camel –

millennia between, and love
and life and death and heavens.

The Visitor

Adonai, Adonai, had you been here...

She searched the convoluted corridors for the ward
among those pale-blue matt-distempered walls;
odour of decay and age, of hurt and weltering humanity
at their pathetic most, foolish, fond and frail

but holding on, with a little salvaged pride,
dull-eyed, with bedpan slack-open mouth,
with spittle dribbling and in half-
embarrassing pyjamas; *Adonai, had you been here...*

She was filled with famine memories, in the grave
baronial workhouse; in silence, save for machinery
throbbing somewhere, she walked heavily
up the deferential stone stairways of sad history;

TV, oxygen, radiators, clock,
the fading, framed pale imitations
of Monet poppies, lilies spreading out on ponds;
the turnip-smells, the disinfectants; *Adonai, Adonai...*

Grapes, seedless of course (his teeth), a bottle
of Lucozade, sunlight through the ward window
glancing off the orange cellophane, a box of Black
Magic (all soft, no toffees). *Oh Adonai...*

The Patient

Back then they had honoured and envied him, king
of the beer-realm, Hilltop Tavern, the good years, decades
when he was lord of his lounge-bar, prince

of the pint-pullers, judge of the spirit-measures,
one eye closed. They came in, late summer nights,
match-wisps of hay in their hair, an age-old thirst

impelling them, the cuckoo-call of the Irish flute
and the mythic scope of the sean-nós telling;
time, gentlemen, please, he would intone, *lads now,*

have ye no homes to go to? No pillows for your heads!
Now he sits in a winged chair, gazing out over the town
where bells are chiming angelus, and he hears *Time!*

Mouth askew, rheum in his eyes, he drools and lolls,
watching through and far beyond the TV screen,
its colours, noise and vibrancy,

for what are they to him now, the soaps and sitcoms?
It is April, frosts lingering, dark birds busy
loading the sycamores with their twig-scrap nests,

but he scarcely notices, winter-chill settled
in his bones, the stiffening joints
throwing mind into confusions; *is it again*

great famine? this the workhouse (its history
of wretchedness, starvation, summer, winter),
for there are hungers, miseries, and he knows them all;

in his head a slow, staccato, sweet replay,
jerky and non-sequential, like those
black-white grey and flickering movies –

Metropolis, *The Best Years of Our Lives* –
that mesmerised him when he sat, open-mouthed,
prepared to walk out through the front gate of his life.

I have been in dread…

since childhood,
        of you, Omnipotent:
Elohim, creator, judge,
        El Elyon, God Most High;

I soared those days
        lithe as a swallow;
I dived into the brown pool,
        finned was I, as a trout,

all body, supple, and glowing flesh;
        but I have been in dread
of you, your arrogant cathedrals, the high
        masquerades of prelates;

God of Mountains, El Shaddai, Adonai,
        YHWH, Unsayable.
But you, Yeshua, as I was, child, in the heat
        and hurry of your youth

did you play? with cousin Yohanan?
        and did you laugh, exult
in the heather slopes?
        Yeshua, Yeshua, Yeshua –

like a mother hushing
        a fretful child, like winds
plushing the lean poplars;
        I have been in dread, Adonai, of you…

The Patient

In the ward, late at night, he cannot sleep; tablets
are single-syllable words he does not understand;

he lies still, watching his grandfather scything hay
in the night-light reflected off the ceiling;

his grandmother churns butter, and he hears
the whurrrp of the plunger, sees her grow

weary; they turn, betimes, to smile at him and why then
should he sleep? There is a hunger

surpassing every hunger, detectable in the eyes,
sometimes in sigh or silence. Midnight the moon –

the ever-so-far-off moon – sends gentle spirits in
and he can almost hear them singing. In darkness

he moves with pleasure through the past, today
is nothing, tomorrow clouded-over with mortality.

He sees himself high in the star-silvered nightscape
moving, naked, among rocks and shadowed boulders,

chilled and touching the unresponding earth,
thrilling to know that if he screams out of excess

of physicality (but he does not) it will make
no difference. Nearing dawn, exhausted, he may touch sleep.

I was acolyte...

exhorted, surpliced
            and shuffle-shoed, taught
    to enter on the altar of God
            who promised joy

    to my green youth. I threw
            stones at a passing bus,
    and ran, skulking and unhappy
            to squat alone, my back

    against an oak, a boy
            confused. And you, Yeshua,
    did you marvel at the snows
            on Hermon? or fling stones

    at the Bedouin trekking through,
            wrapped in themselves,
    their caravans passing, irksome,
            like days, like seasons,

out to the desolate rock valleys?
            And did you skulk, lonely,
in some olive grove –
            or could you hear, down all the centuries,

a boy like me, murmuring
            Latin prayers into the air:
introibo ad altare Dei…
            and did you prophesy the mess of pain,

hear your death cry,
            suffer already your confusion,
your short
            life?

The Patient

Afternoon sometimes when he lies in bed
and even the birds fall silent, in the ward
sunlight drifts across and he thinks of those
bright lights that might have been; often

the unregarded moments surface, the small
possibilities of perfection, that now are merely
multitudes of candle flames scarce visible
against the day. He was young a while,

has been old a long, long time. All those evenings,
just he, and she, in quiet together by the firelight,
sleep creeping up to them like a purring cat, he knows
were a contentment scarcely treasured. He counts

the grace-filled times he knew with her, and they, too,
are multitudes, a long music that almost
got it right. He sighs, distressed, contented. Aware
that it is enough; it is more than enough.

The Visitor

She thinks how he could not dance, but stood
camel-stiff and swaying. She –
moving with joy in astonishment at his youth –

waltzed their sharing of warm red wine
on the beaches of Gascony, and tangoed with him
from one Greek island to the next

under a passion-fruit, unclouded sky. Now he sits
lost, unseeing, in that old-earth smell of dying,
and though she takes his hand, fondling it, it lies

trembling, between hers, and unresponsive.
The music, she thinks, has faded though a sustained
note, profoundly beautiful, persists. His old age

is decrepit but she believes a carefree angel hovers
close above them. She would waltz still (were her body
not stiff and heavy, too) though their life together

is done, and pain holds silently between. He is gone
somewhere into the dark though she knows there are white
horses stomping in a spring meadow, attending him,

and the meadowbank where he walks without her
is rich in the blue of wild anemone. These days
patches of snow on the iron mountain have almost

melted; soon the cuckoo will make dells of the valley
and the wrens are singing wildly already
among the dancing thorns of the haw.

The Patient

He sits, hours, in the winged chair,
mind (when capable) sifting a life, the dark
passageways of unbelief, belief.

We have need again of good
news, he thinks, eyes glazed over
sore and slow-weeping, chin

dropped onto the grey-hair top
of his chest. Times he thinks he has seen
God, though his vision blurred;

he has made inquiries everywhere, everywhere
he has sought God's face. Now
Mozart's sweet concerto for alto clarinet

is playing on the radio, music
of life's underground heart-beat, larksong
high above the treetops. Once he saw

a brown owl pass among the trees
in disconcerting silence. April. April again.
What is it he has been searching for?

At the small desk...

where I gouged in
        my initials, already
the words were loud: *Thou shalt love
        the Lord thy God...*

Love. A word, Yeshua,
        like so many others
to be swallowed down,
        like pills. But I have need

of you, have been translating
          all the words into sunlight,
days when the black-and-gold-striped
          bumblebees were busy

through the fuchsia flowers, and we –
          small boys mesmerised, sitting
in a circle on the earth –
          sang *t á tá síne fada ar an á* –

and I watched the seagull's wings
          translucent, shiverful
against the cobalt sky. And you, Yeshua,
          were nothing, a sound,

an argument, a rule. And who,
          the Brother asked, who made the world?
God made the world, we shouted
          and Brother handed out the reader,

and oh that paper-smell,
          the new, clean cover and within!
all the world's secrets
          soon to be revealed. I heard

the scolding reiterated
          ratcheting from the corncrake;
the world of caterpillar, heather, lark,
          of bicycle wheels and that

flush of blue from speedwell
          in under the hawthorn bush,
took all I had of adoration.
          Now I am entering

on the darkest gulley. I have much
          to say to her I love. My heart
strains with contentment
          and frustration. Light dims. A chill

rises. We wallow long
      in the soft–mud pond
of our selfhood.
            I would live it all again

with her, if she would, I would tell her so,
            could I move my lips. Under intolerable
weight of the sheets my body dances for her
            and my spirit sings. She is, has been, magnificent.

The Visitor

She was sitting by the bed, imagining a sound
to distract her: waves breaking against a Gascon shore
and he, lithe and elegant, running on the sand
to shake the sea-drops from his skin; almost
perfect in his flesh. How he ran back to her,
kissed her with that salted tongue, and laughed. Now
he has moved away from her again, aged
and broken, held together (on the noiseless shore
of eternity) by tube and drip and monitor,
eyes closed, breathing harsh so that she grows
afraid of him, curtains drawn about them, he
already something other, somewhere else, she knows
he will not wake, he will not return. She shifts, frightened,
moves out into the corridor. Oh Adonai, oh Adonai.

I spent hours…

      by the lake, pushing small sticks out
            and they carried my unshaped dreams –
the waves pushing them ever back,
            unworded dreams, and ghosts to come…

You, too, young Jewish boy, stooped
            at the lake's edge, bemused perhaps in the old

36

covenant breezes, the hot, demanding landscape
        lifting to barren hills; while here the rain

made sodden the track to my lake-shore,
        played water-flower music where little birds
whistled in the reeds. I am caught in the storms
        of a different covenant. The distances

incomprehensible, my wish for friendship with you
        unreasonable. You, too, stood in the shallows
watching towards a far-off shore, your feet
        deliciously disturbing sand, you, too,

in love with the earth, its teeming harmonies,
        the russets, the finches, the weathers... and watched
while Miryam washed the clothes and hummed
        out by the stone troughs; I, at mother's knee,

colouring in the pages with thick-stubbed crayons,
        scarlet for the bush on fire, green-blue the Red
Sea, white the foam on the waves' parting, red again
        for the drowning chariots, the Egyptian blood.

I see you, Yeshua, whittling a branch, the bark
        falling at your feet like whipped-off strips of flesh;
and did you shape a sling? or catapult? as I did,
        using the letter Y, as I did, in the hunt for birds,

the innocent psalm-singers, while the stones flew
        across the winds, our child-hands learning how to lift
from earth the rough-edged matter, seeking our prey,
        willing to destroy. Regrets, Yeshua. Such regrets...

The Widow

There are, inside my head, cathedral spaces,
coigns of cross-grained stone-light, cornucopias
of many-coloured stain; I have known, with him, cathedral

happiness, and now, cathedral loss. We are made
not less than angels but I have knelt
beneath tall stone-draped Seraphim and found

word and prayer stone-bound: *To whom God's love...*
I should have stayed, and held his hand, then
kissed those parching lips, that white-schist brow

but I was scared: the needles, tubes, the monitors...
Perhaps he might have sensed my love,
that he was not alone, taking that dreadfilled step...

The clogging rituals of death have left
terror, like a tumour, swollen within me; what if
there is no forgiveness for our birthing? what if

the tenderness of Christ is fraud? Now gravid hands
have rested on my shoulders to emphasise
my new place in this charnel world. I walked

amongst weeds and wilderness by the parkside pond;
eye of the goldeneye, claw of the water-rail, a rat
gone dunking down the hollowed heart of a tree;

a heron, rakish-thin, stood above me
as Donne the preacher might have stood
admonishing. He who is beggar, who would be

governor, came knocking to the door; suave and discrete
in light blue shirt, pink tie and golfer cufflinks,
he was braced with promises and gorgeous lies

bristling like nostril-hairs, like down-tufts in his ears:
Is it a small thing, I asked him, that on your watch
the people's bones lie bleaching in the sun? This

is my country where I have loved, and lost; and you
still hectoring. Because you are ashamed of God, because
you have been paid in cash and you will thrive, a while,

for yet a very little while. He smiled. He shook his head. Ireland.
Isaiah, it is said, was a little man, balding,
fist knuckling to his head to hide embarrassment,

yet was he of the people; one lazy eye could see
down the corridor of centuries, how the child, uncouth
and cradled in a crib, would start to burn all flesh

to the purest nib, and you deny him, conscious
of your bank account and honour in your seat. I closed
the door, softly, as he turned, walked down the drive

and knocked, smiling, at the next door. My love is dead;
I found unholy dread of that dark bourne and feared
lest he suddenly come back, lest his hand

reach up to clasp on mine, or his eyes open
that had witnessed horror absolute. Now I claim
new ignorance; briars have reached in

over the garden walls, outgrown bushes
overshade the jasmine; a blackbird
is sitting solemn in the high poplars, almost

motionless, not stirred to sing; but I will wait
dream-rich in memory, with what is left in the wild
garden, a love-light, music, and the dream of Christ.

IV

Rain Falling in the Far West

I

I am standing, old and self-absorbed as Lear,
out on bogland, where I started;
there are skylarks, pipits, black-monk crows

and plover, secret in the heathers, calling; dried blood
on the scraws, gnawed gristle,
furred creatures cowering, the raptor hawk;

where have I been, all these years, far from myself?
Soft rains drift in mist-shapes
shading everything to grey; I would hear the voices

of those I have loved and lost, I standing now on the brink.
Of Aquinas at the last they said
that he was laying down the instruments

of his writing; what I have done
feels like turf-dust. What is there left, but spirit?

II

Rain is falling in the far west, as it has ever fallen.
Easy to miss the star against the city lights
and shoppers; here, on bogland, is a side-aisle quiet,

where nothing extraordinary happens, where you may accept
emptiness and the cotton-quivering
of a solitary self; here, too, the harrier is close, what is eternal

hovers, it is the dread festival of God's descent
into the flesh, his presence
in the ongoing history, heart in hiding, forever

beginning. The night is still and clear under frost, great clouds
passing, slow, relentless; an ocean-full
of stars, a cradle moon, and in the windows of the houses

candles lighting; sweet shiver-glass of ice
on the bogpools, and one great light reflecting.

III

Wild honey hides among the combed roots, in the dark
it scents the air. Childheart,
I was told the bleak mythologies of black-bog waters: the giant

otter in the pools, black-souled goblin with his storm lamp,
and Clovenhoof himself, ready to reach
a leathery claw out of mud to take your ankle; there would be

fear, and fascination, there would be danger, stumbling, a fall.
In the far west rain is falling; there is epiphany
in the movement of a fox, long-fellow, sleek, a languid

lovely-loping, orange-brown body slipping through
brown-orange growth; in the soft
dew-gentled dawn, the spread-out jewellery of gossamer webs

shivers silver in destructibility;
the heathers, too, ripple in the breeze, like water.

IV

I put my ear down close to the bog-earth
roots, to hear
the heartbeat of the magma;

there are no hard edges in the peatland,
no table-corners,
cupboard-doors, car-boot-sharpness; I am in love

with earth, the various, the lovely, though
it is not home: for it is written –
God so loved the world... I stand

on the wallow-surface of belief, winds from the sea
taking my breath away;
the paths across the bog lead always on

further into bog, then
stop. Nowhere. Where God is.

V

Here is no locked tabernacle; God exults, in frochan,
bilberry root. Here is no church, stone-built,
no steeple proud in its piercing of the skies; sometimes

a dragonfly, its rainbow gossamer wings, passes by
low over the cottons; I can kneel
on sphagnum moss, its soft green sponge, to ask forgiveness

because resurrection is ongoing; curlew calls, alleluia; and still
all of the bogland is in motion, bleached bones
of elk and wolf and hare, rising inexorably towards the surface.

Bell rings for angelus, the stooping figures rise and stand a while
in the transept of eternity. Rain
is falling in the far west, as it has ever fallen; in the windows

candles lighting;
what is there left, now, but spirit?

November

Again the parlour has filled to overflowing
with the beloved dead – and I

stand distraught outside the great blurred window
looking in; little light where I am,

a soft persistent starlight; where they are, there are chandeliers,
though the dead are distant, a little

indistinct; they have been blown, perhaps, through the open door
into the hallway, like those several

beautifully-veined and parti-coloured leaves, old gold and scarlet,
from the trees that stand

bereft of summer, bare-head to the chilled and chilling
sky; and have wandered in

through that other door we never opened, and though they are
a little ruffled at the edges, a little

sere, they are upright and lightly swaying, the best crystal
in their hands; grandfather, possibly,

in the far corner, by the walnut cabinet, a vague
moustachioed figure; Nanna, wearing

her best of smiles, serving; closer, by the oil-lamp,
motherfather, fathermother, relishing –

as they never did before – a happy foolishness; closer still,
behind the net-curtained window, my

brother, cured of all ills, and laughing; there is a shadowy
and shrouded host-like figure

moving quietly amongst them, greeting them all with a little
banter. Ah well, we have allowed them

this one month to be amongst us, this first mustering
of winter, as if they were not always there

before our consciousness, calling out against our grieving.

Release

You may follow the river's
idiosyncratic ways, across reedy meadows,
under the rough-stone arches
where finger-sized golden eels will linger in the flow –

all the way down to the shore;
scatterings of clinker-wood and varnished boats
are held by seaweed-weighted ropes
to the stout and pitch-painted piles of the kesh;

the easy-lifting waves
break in their soiled-white suds against the keels, and the oars
clatter in their rowlocks like strong
arms rattling iron bars; here you may relish

the heave and sigh of your griefs
telling again of your loss and how very well you have been loved.
Stand still a while,
acknowledging the sharp winds coming off the sea

troubling the boats; you may
shiver a moment, conscious of enormous space before you; now,
should you half-close your eyes
you may glimpse them (those whom you call to your care

from the sudden discovery
of a hand-written postcard marking an old book), they are
agitated and impatient that you
turn at last and release them, out over the great expanses

towards the furthest visible horizon, and they
will never glance back towards you, as you make your way home
under rough-stone arches, across
reedy meadows, following the river's idiosyncratic ways.

Workshop

In grandfather's work shed there was only
a heavybreathing flickering oil-lamp;

the old man worked, planing and chiselling, his jaws
clenched; I touched, under caution, vice and pliers,

and loved the lacelike, incandescent light.
His big hands were callused, but his fingers toiled

with a feminine delicacy; he wore a waistcoat
stiff with wood-dust, a collarless shirt, a stud

dangling. Times now when I slip in among the dead
to let the memories sustain me, I will focus

on old certainties, and – being a ghost – observe
with the sharpened tools of listening; I wish to be

instrument for the chiselling of words, telling the old
story. Translating it. Often with a fine failure, sometimes

delicately true, and keeping faith. At work. Witness.
Still taken by the lacelike, incandescent light.

Museum of Country Life

Turlough, Castlebar, Co. Mayo

On the hither bank of the dark river, Methuselah-Heron stood,
the flow of minute, nor day, nor season
bothering him; this side the river, Patrick's high round tower

guards the dead against all weathering; across the water
the demesne, Big House, where I take the lift
(chrome fittings, engaging mirror) down out of the present, step

out into Granny's scullery, and there she is! sitting on a wobbledy
three-leggedy stool, the hour-glass churn
held like an unwilling child between her knees; black apron

with its smattering of stars, her grey hair wisping on her heated face,
and she plunges and plunges,
churning; there is buttermilk in the bruised enamel bucket

where I dip a chipped Irel-coffee porringer to drink; on the floor
last night's scoured-out rose-patterned chamber-pot,
on the shelf tureens with grey-blue willows, eternal flight

of rust-brown swallows on a rust-brown sky. 'Run,' she tells me,
'tell Granddad the spuds are in the pot'; I make,
gently, soft-heel, genteel half-turns and there I am at once, away

beyond the crossroads at Cafferky's roadside forge, big mule Romeo
heaving at the ropes; Granddad
has his big fob watch, he has opened the jacket

of his RIC uniform, smoking his white clay pipe and packing
tobacco down
with his big hard thumb;
he points, saying the words for me, tongs, croppers, hammers

and there – collar and hames, bridle and reins; we are standing hot
in a racket-hall livid with fire, there is anvil-ding and
hiss-swish-swash of steam when the red-hot shoe is whooshing down

into the basin, and misery! the sudden wuthering roar of the ass;
Cafferky, small and skinny, grinning nails,
is sporting his liver-coloured leathern apron to withstand all wars;

'Have you done,' says Granddad, spitting down into the flames,
'your homework?' and I make, gently, soft-heel genteel
half-turns, and there I am in the Achill schoolroom, nailed boots

and rolled-down socks, trousers to the knee, all us boys awed
before the expanse of the world beyond,
slates and chalk on the long desks, nib and inkwell and headline

copybooks, and I will forge out words, plunge deep into language,
I will fill copies, and pattern sentences into shape
in stitched and covered books. I was born here, will die, but will be

forever. I took the lift again, reluctantly, up to the present. Outside,
a long-eared owl let out its cry, obstinate
as a rusty hinge, from a high branch in the age-old pines.

Still Life

for Jane O'Malley

Often I stand abstracted, as if stilled before a painting,
in the scullery of the old yellow house –
sunlight on the whitewashed walls, an ochre stain

dribbled from the tap down the stone sink – and touch again
the love I knew from my gentlewoman granny, a radiance
held in the crock, the porringer, the oven glove, the churn,

there as she had left them, placed, and not abandoned,
though she is gone, and the objects gone, and the house
a haunting-place for spectres. I pass back into her world

and see, again, her well-filled missal, memoriam cards, pressed
faded forget-me-not between the pages, and sense a fragrance
from freesia she arranged in a vase upon the windowsill. Still

life, epiphanies of remembered love, all solid things
redeeming us though we stand silent, helpless, and in hope.

Night Prayer

Rembrandt: *Landscape with the Rest on the Flight into Egypt*

I

This, too, you see, is prayer, these words I labour to admit
    under the spirit's prompting, words on the notebook
    difficult to decipher, the ink flowing out too fast

in the first stirrings; pen, copybook and keyboard
    in an attempt to touch the source of light,
    of life, the groundwork of our hope. Here, too,

II

figures in a nightscape, a pause in the difficult journey; questions
    of resting in penumbra, of knowing light is fragile,
    like a child holding its greedy mouth to the breast;

there is a fire of sticks, trouvaille of twig and branch, to keep
    wolves at bay (between here and destination, Emmaus, say,
    beyond a life's full circle, light against the darkness) and this

III

is Jesus, name and nature of our source and sustenance, this
    is God, dwarfed by trees and distances, enormous landscape
    and a darkening night, and you grow aware that here

the watchful small lamps of greed and power are looming over all.
    The canvas, too, is prayer, impasto, brush and palette knife,
    working to ease the blackness about the light, cognisant

of the death of innocents; it is all self-portrait, still life, a halt
   in the hastening, the helplessness of humankind before its own,
   the helplessness of God trusting Himself to flesh;

love is a small child, far from consciousness, hunted; should he be
   found and killed, what then? what then? Rembrandt
   knew that distance between himself and God — all time, all space,
                                                                    all

V

life, all death — had been too great; the instruments of art, sharpened and
   softened in the desiring heart, shorten the distance, finding
   a sheltering tree, light shouldering the darkness; this

Egypt of the imagination, this den of safety called
   exile, as world with its instruments of power and economics
   preys on you and how can you believe your pigments

VI

touch beyond impossibility? Image, less real than
   thistledown in a western gale, less permanent than golden light
   reflected on a pond, you try to empty the ocean of silence

with the holding power of pigments, the silence that is God.
   Christ-beyond-all-grasping, the heart in its pleading is a series
   of shifting darkscapes, vaulted in night-prayer passageways.

Paul, the Apostle, Told

how he was lifted into Paradise, discovering
things of which no man might speak; his words
flew in circles about his Christ,
small birds fastened by the frailest thread.

Greenfinch
hesitate now by the bird table, their wheezing song
welcome, for here
in January weathering, stone, rain and clayclod

make dismal harmonies; this
is Ireland, its dirge and requiem, its adagio.
I have been sending words,
like feathers tied with wax, out

towards the country's heart, learning
it takes years to fly
across the space between one man
and another. Off the marsh road,

in a field beyond a field, a flock
of stray, high-stepping cranes, grave demoiselles,
moves in slow ballet across the wet,
because the earth on which they deign to walk –

though tarnished, tarnishing – is yielding life. Paul
could never tell, for sure,
whether his flight was in or out of body.
And always, in my mind,

Icarus stands aggrieved, wax wings raised in preparation,
waiting for the breeze
that will lift him out of flesh
into the gorgeous sun.

Guardian

Whispers within the tunnels of the bone. A sudden thought,
from the goose-pimples on the skin. Therefore I hold to
the long, reaching arms of God's embrace so whole
they make an angel, shadow following everywhere
by day and night; it will be, at times, obliterating
snowfalls of care, a force eleven Atlantic storm
of love. I shudder at it and am scared
by such a generosity. And I
demand more. Will die
for it. Die
hugely.

The Swallow

You grow – like flowers from their soil –
    from the name and notion of your heart-place:
    Bunnacurry, Achill, Mayo; you are listening

– at the fleshly distance – to the music
    of the teeming hours, the prophecies;
    you dissipate, though slowly, what has been your essence

until you turn again, prodigal after years, on your journey
    back towards truth: the escallonia hedge, the baby-wail
    of the out-of-the-vertical back gate,

and to father, decades dead, watching. Now you stand
    at the harvesting of what has been
    the wild acres, terrified at the suddenness

of the years' passing, your quick tock-tick
    out of uncountable millennia, here at this damp meadow-edge
    to marvel at the swallow that has swooped across you

low over the meadow, that flash
    of red-rust feathers on the throat, and it is gone
    in a fling of its wings off up beyond the ash-tree hedge;

you write it down, then, in wonder, in words
    that are nets of air that cannot hold
    the mystery. You are working now towards silence,

admitting the absence of your father though he is still
    present in phlox and ox-eye daisy, how you are –
    in this one moment – clothed again in home, become

the breeze beneath the swallow's wings, become
    the sky, the murdered insect, the swallow,
    become the prophecy and become, almost, the music.

In the Margins

The day he reached, furtively,
into his inside pocket and showed me

my poem cut from the newspaper, was the day
I knew I loved him. I remembered

watching him in the brown-dark, stuffy office,
there by the seaweed reaches of Achill Sound,

while his pen scratched uneasily across
official forms, though his mind, I knew,

was on the rocks beyond Purteen
where the mackerel shoaled, where the seal

lifted its head heavy with water-wisdom
to take him in. When he finished with the form

he laid aside the pen, held a match
to a stump of red wax, as if he signed

some easy-going labourer's doom with a drop
of his own blood. At home, in the margins

of his books – Gorky, Goethe, Proust –
his notes and exclamations trailed and turned

like the irascible and business-like marking out
of ants in their tasks and traffickings; and always

in the breast pocket of his jacket, two pens
visible, the plump and easy-tempered

fountain pen and the biro, slim-fit, fast to the threads
of the imagination. To whom I owe the steady

application to the word, the flourished signing of my name,
as if I had captured some quick creature in the net.

Driftwood

What do you say to the dying, when already
they have waded out beyond hearing
towards a place you have not earned the right
to enter – *good-bye: farewell:* or *God be with you?*

Or do you, as did I then, sit silent, hurt
by the impenetrable fact of *his*
dying? who held me safe on the water,
who promised he would not leave me

floundering. But he disappeared, into breaking
waves, I steadfast on the long strand, watching
the shivering chevron shape the greylag make
leaving these shores, and what I heard from them

sounded like crying, a fading dirge for the seasons,
a music of inner, inevitable need. Otherwise
silt, and courage failing; otherwise only the so-far
written lines, the words like driftwood to cling to.

John Clare's Bedlam

What do they pack for you in that battered suitcase
as they leave you to the madhouse door? How do they say

'goodbye'? how turn away? And how do you
turn from them, from the finches, from the sloe-

blossoms and music of the rainclouds – how do you face
towards that scanting cell? How will the warm sun's rays

discover where you are, all this not in the scheme
of God's devising? Can you sing while you suffer the severe

processes they have planned for your purgation?
– bleedings, chemicals – to turn the runnels of your brain

to oozings? And all the while the unfazed robin
calls you to rake for her the good, black earth again,

the fox would lead you down his trodden path, through
fragrances of pine, the tough-branched undergrowth you know

out to the heather marches where you would hymn, apart,
God and made-things, Christ and abundance, because the heart

is a shire too great to be enclosed, and the sky above is chaste
and shiftful as divinity, life-giving as the dark blood of the Christ.

Tracks

I have been taking the slow steam train
      out of Westport, through Newport and Mulranny
      to Achill Sound; the rickety toy-town carriages
      sing adventure, the other all-swavering souls

insubstantial as I. Embarrassing
      backyards, knickers, vests and underpants
      heist themselves shamelessly into the winds
      while the far-off Néifins sing of the purity

of leaf, of the upland downland shivering
      deserts of the West, till we come rocking
      over the russet-rich, the sandstone cloud-high
      viaduct into Newport. Pause, to steam a little,

to gather puff, then face out past the dull back-ends
      of business, green-slime ribbons dirtying old walls,
      allsouls together refreshed on lemonade and spirits;
      out over the pool where father in his dream-days

stood fly-fishing, content and timeless, sea-trout
      playing tig with him, and winning. We are delayed,
      Mulranny hill, behind the gap-toothed Great Southern Hotel;
      they are taking on more water, while wallowing below us

the scattered islands of Clew Bay, the sacred mountain
      reaching like a pyramid into clouds; there's a sudden
      suspiration, emigrants passing us by in the sibilant
      sorrowing of a rainshower over the most lush

rhododendrons; a soul lowers a window and the scent
      of the far West – of rain and heather and hearthstone –
      sunders the heart once more. Now we are waltzing
      along the quiet inlet of the sea, a kestrel hovers

against the dark-green shoulder-blades of Tonragee,
      by hawthorn villages and fuchsia glades, Slieve More
      growing slowly visible and urging tears, for this is
      ghost-journeying, the longed-for resurrected essence

of a past so often prayed elegant enough to redeem us, imagination
   ruefully setting by the negatives – while we glide – shunting
   into Achill Sound, and halt, juddering; so many

                                        ghost-companions
   about me still, and so much loneliness.

Genova, Italia

i.m. Edoardo Sanguineti

It may be possible, from this port city,
to set out across the known and the new
worlds, your masted galleon under sail again;

black-cassocked priests walk slowly out on the piazza
where the water-sculptures rise, and hymn, and fall;

you hear the footsteps, across the streets, of the poet
who dressed his joy in life in mourning black,
sent postcards back from native and exotic cities
coloured with his pastel messages of love; now

in the Ducal Palace, under monstrous chandeliers,
ordinary man lifts up espressos to the gods, breathes
deeply here, inhaling stillness, the heart

filling, as the sails do, till you find yourself
at peace, riding on billows of air towards home.

V

The Summer of 2010

for Ursula

I have considered, often, how it might be:
turning in again at the red gate, you
and I, no more aged than we were then but just
as passionate, when it was April in the world,

when our carrier-bags of grief were empty
as they were when we first touched, that night
under the streetlamp in the smalltown square;
I have considered, too, how I would want to be

so still the kestrel knows me as rock or bush
as he hangs like the searing eye of God
over the heartland, I want to think that all of flesh
is cohort and endearing as the magenta beads

of our fragrant heathers. The canterbury bells
you planted, the digitalis, the geraniums
are spreading their living colours before our window;
our dead, who have held their sorrowing

steadily against us, have moved on into their own
ideal orchards and we stand now, at peace together,
watching in awed astonishment how the eucalyptus
that we set down stands high in guardianship,

how a young child's voice calls out with joy
discovering orchids in the wild meadow: I see it all
as a music, rich as the great ninth symphony, the rhythms
inexorable, the key D minor, the harmonies assured.

The Shower

And wasn't it something, after all, to be caught like that,
out in the world without coat or mac or brolly, foolish
in this our country? And taking refuge in a stand of trees,
rain plushing through the leaves and branches over you

and coming down in slow and generous drops and plops
missing you some of the time, sometimes not, and the sound
like a roomful of silent readers turning their pages all
together, till you felt embraced in your smallness

by the fragrance of rain over leaf-mould, by the green
darkness that held you, and the world out there so all
riven with grandeur and greyness that the drip drip drip

on your unprotected shoulder was the tap tap tap of someone
reminding you, just that, lest you forget, lest you take it
for granted: so you are glad you were unreasonable, unprepared.

Heron

As it was in the beginning, archaeopteryx, or
as close to it as
feathers, wishbone, bonytail and teeth.

Learning to mind its own business
in the claw-and-jaw
world of dinosaurs. Phoenix-Heron, recreating itself

in the sacred precincts of the sun-god Ra; self
as the recurrent
rising of the Nile, as resurrection, self as sun. Flew

awkwardly – such a gangly pair – into the high
heron-haven corner
of the Ark, and creaked as the timbers creaked, the waters lifting;

in the marginalia of scroll, papyrus, and epistle
Heron stands, eremite,
wonder-bird heavy with weight of the millennia. Sepulchral,

like the groaner Jeremiah, like the scrawny-limbed
Anthony of the desert;
intent, like Scotus, like Coleridge, Arnold, Pound, like Yeats.

★

Here, now, it is spring, in a Dublin park; among small islands
of the lesser celandine,
under the pussy-willow's catkin-fluffy spread, mallard

clump on mud and their own dumped droppings, male
in the opulence
of extravagant colours, his mate, all brown and dun and everyday,

dull in incipient drudgery towards birthing; and there,
high in the barely greening
branches of the sycamore, Seán Gaunt Heron

constructs his twiggery, sticks to make a home like a collapsing
Japanese washitsu,
good for his lady and puffed-out ugly young, for this

emperor and empress of the world. It is young-year, in effervescent
and ever-recurring freshness
startling us back where we would dwell again

★

fat with promise. One day of languid mist,
(an age ago) I was out
in the pine-grove, with catapult (constructed from a Y

of branching furze, tough rubber band, and leather holding), stones
in my pocket, slaughter in my heart –
young hunter-gatherer, wee primitive, stalking a heron

high among the Scots-pine trees; till a feather, dark-grey, splayed,
spilled slowly down
and when I snatched at it, it touched me gently, in soft

reprimand; a sudden downpour made me hide
in against the bark
and I stood chastened, stilled and very much alone.

★

Heron-haven, as it was in the beginning, and now
this eldering
man-face is full of hours, the eyes bulging bilging

and the stubble of the beard most difficult to harrow
as the lines of the years
thicken with regrets, harden with loss while all the words

begin to lumpen on the chapped tongue, lose their once svelte
quickness, and fall
to creaking sounds like old dry timbers when the pith begins

to fall away, like moulted feathers, like memory – original silence
settling slowly back, around me
here under the heavens, across the landscape, wuthering.

Burial

They were washed out, sea–cow and
ocean-elephant, on a spit of sand,

curvaceous beauties of the toughest hides
whose ballet in the emerald depths has ended;

they lie, mysteries on the foreshore, that have been
elegantissimi in the fashions of the sea, sailing

as underwater caravels on the spice-trails
towards salt cities and crusted fortresses carved

out of green and white-flagged waves; and we,
who stand apart, aggrieved against the stench,

catch at our breath, bring our oil-leaking diggers down
to bucket great holes into the weeping earth.

Seán Gaunt Heron

He was standing tall in heron rectitude,
      blue-grey frock-coat and tails,
      duine le Día and squireen, in ragged britches attaining

elegance, poised, too, and deadly. I stood,
      still as he, watching, as if we could ever make
      meaningful contact; the focus of his yellow eye

turned on me, the long neck folding slowly down
      into the shadows of himself, polite, you'd think, like an old
      retainer, the black wisps of his feather-crest

graceful as an elder knight's, but I knew his watchfulness
      was out of long experience, flight the better part
      of fortitude, for he was here, saucy (among the riff-raff

slatternly humans) forced in out of the damaged wild,
      sharing the city pond with coot and water-hen,
      so I moved cautiously, allowing him his space;

he, too, is facing down hard times, his origin
      and his future, just like ours, being one, so I offered
      homage to the countless generations

contained in that thin body, to the elusive
      mystery of heron-hood, our legendary-grown
      great-grandpa heron, haughty still, survivor.

Wherefore art thou Romeo?

Morning. After soft, Irish rain; my first day responsible
   for bringing home the turf,
      taking the old ass, Romeo, from the stable,

finagling him, harnessing, halter, bridle, bit...
   There was a dust-familiar smell
      from his hirsute donkey-ness, big ears flapping

like darned socks upon a line, ragged-roped tail
   flicking at flies, the belly-band
      holding wicker-basket creels on either flank.

*

What a setting out it was into bright morning!
   Don Quixote on his Rocinante,
      or rather Sancho Panza on his mule – me cocked up

on his bone-hard rump, erratic trot trot tripple trot
   along the tarmacadam road, king
      of the universe, young man-with-purpose, labouring

towards legend. I had been day-dreaming as we came,
   Brother Ass and I,
      down off the road, along the turf-mould track

across the bog: the gathering home of small chateaux of peat.
   Bluebottles – glozing on old flesh – incandescent
      cobalt spit-balls, whuzzed up angrily when I kicked

what I thought was a sod, and I recoiled, half sickened
   by stench and empty eye-sockets,
      the wet-sleek rictus of the thing – learning ancient

bogland secrecies, how the heather beauties of peatland hold
   soggy purses of putrefaction in the black
      waterpools that slow, and ever-so, create their treasure.

I filled the creels from the turf clamp, sod upon sod, dry
    and hard, with the fragrance of heather
        and the twisted dead-roots of vanished deal and oak;

Romeo stood, head bowed, in contemplation of the patterned carpeting
    of the mother-bog. Sweat
        soon in my eyes, the palms of my hands stippled into hurt,

my back aching; until, on the way home, I was one again
    with donkey, with the sorrowing of plod
        and burden, one in the weariness, in the love of the living

thistle, of ragwort, bog-cotton, one perhaps in the desire to lift
    out of heaviness and to gambol
        somersaulting across blue meadows of the sky...

But we tramped onwards, morning already turned
    towards the soft-tone terminal of noon.
        The long afternoon would be tedious in its repetitions;

I had come to know the only way over a rough-stone bog-track
    is to balance all delights and sorrows
        the way we pack the sods of turf in wicker creels

either side of the grumpy ass: Romeo, beast and legend,
    for there was one entered Yerushalayim
        in triumph, riding the bone-hard rump of an ass...

By early evening a ruby glow from the lowering sun was warming
  the whitewashed wall by the grove;
      I heard, from his paddock, Romeo cry out

that donkey-roar of earth-depression, that heartbreak call
  rising high in a frame of anguish and sinking
      back into his mocked and burden-bearing flesh;

I watched him then, from over the paddock fence; held himself
  still, head down, in a brown study
      though I could see the eyes, wide and wild, and the penis

swollen as a black sock bulged with wet sand; ears rose, tail
  twitched and then he was off,
      clearing the wooden gate and skittering across the yard,

out over the road and away towards the village, racing
  down the fuchsia lane, by Slattery's
      slaughter-house where sheep-carcasses hung

on iron hooks, their blood drup-dripping into enamel buckets,
  until he disappeared – a racehorse,
      and I, laboured, following – round O'Grady's bend.

Where three lanes meet I found him, in a small stand of alders,
  stilled again, head down, and docile;
      he followed, hooves slipping on the gravel surfaces,

and if I clout him hard on that boned rump, what would that be?
                                                    addition
      to his incomprehension, anger
          at my own inadequacies, my frustrations. I shut him

in his stable, watched him for a while, Romeo, spent
  from the day, contented. The light had left
      the whitewashed wall, speckles of dirt and mould, like
                                              hints of night

were visible; I stood, stilled by wonder as a many-legged zig-zag thing
       raced at an angle down the stippled surface;
              and was cold suddenly, something about responsibility,
                                                              something

of need much greater than I could understand, child's soul confused
       and opened, part of it, outside of it, turning indoors
              to family, and prayers, to the easy embrace of sleep.

Eucalyptus

for Francis Harvey

For many years the humming eucalyptus
offered abiding-places amongst its branches

in a warm and wind-wild festivity of foliage;
now, after prolonged snowfalls, after the murdering

frosts of winter, it is standing, dead. Scentless. Sounds
like dry skins rubbing against each other. The leaves

vanished, though in spring and everywhere around
trees and bushes reach again in baby-green,

vociferous in branch and foliage, and playful
in the breeze. The eucalyptus, not being family,

succumbed to this winter's persistent sorrowing.
Its bark has cracked, patchy in brown, it shrivels

and peels off, like an old man's wrinkled skin;
and I am remembering how the stars

played hide-and-seek amongst its leaves, how sometimes
the moon was lodged in its nets of branches.

What I am afraid of now is that the eucalyptus –
after it is felled and its dried-out bones have been

tossed into our stoves and fireplaces – will forget us,
forget how it sheltered, how it fed our several senses

and that all that will be left to us is a stump,
bland and featureless, like a once-familiar name.

The Seal

Night fell in a cacophony of storms,
winds and rains
smashing against the house and rattling
anything remotely loose –
the side-gate, the stable-door-latch, the pantry window –

suggesting how we are always on the lip
of original chaos and the mud-treacherous
downward slope of time.
Morning dawned to a psalmody of calm,
no breeze, scarce one

wool-bud cloud against the sky.
I came upon a seal, beached, there
as if resting from its long sea-labours, and I approached
with caution, lest I disturb;
sweet-salt stench

was already thickening the air, this castaway
waiting for its lover ocean to come and take it back
into its bosom. Sirach says
when a human being finishes she is just
beginning, and when she stops

she is still perplexed.
And what of seals? born to it, that swift
gambolling like flight, that lissom slaughtering, at times
head and whiskers popping up to watch
peculiar doings of the humans

passing time
noisy and wasteful at the sea's edge;
I watched as a black-backed gull
hopped guiltily sideways towards the carcass, this
retired Seafarer, this Ancient Mariner...

But where I stood,
at the furthest edge of Europe, at the hither-rim
of the utter ocean,
I fancied I could hear
a slow-drawn long-held sigh:

as if the ever-generous murderous sea had grown aware
of some contagion in its depths. Sirach says:
like a drop of water from the sea,
like a grain of sand from the seashore, so are a few years
among the days of eternity.

VI

Dead Weight

Late autumn, the gardens lay as if oppressed, hydrangeas
like the raked-through grey of Granny's hair, her shoulders
slumped. I stood before the grotto, those images of suffering
and the helpless reach of mourning, darkened further

after a fall of rain; the path through the novitiate grounds
was slippery, with bleak and yellow leaves, but I was out
praying the Little Office, whispering lauds, *you make
the winds your messengers, you lift us up* – I prayed –

on the wings of eagles. I knew, mid-morning, the inhaled
exhaled pleasures of isolation, my as-yet-child's heart
open to the Spirit's breathing. But the farm Brother called,
beckoning me to the shed; soutane discarded, he stood

in a dirt-smeared vest, grasping a sheep, her wool a raked-
through grey, her hooves skittering in terror on the stone floor;
'hold her tight, lad, tight', he told me; I left my book –
its delicate gilt-edged pages, the red silk bookmarks – down,

and held her, felt the body juddering, saw the amber eye widening
till the Brother touched the humane killer to her skull, fired
and I knew the sudden desperate dead weight
that dragged me down on top of her dreadfully still, hot, body.

A Fledgling Saint

In the long, hushed library of the seminary
I was copying out the signs and signals

left littered across our spirit-scapes by the busy
Fathers of the Church: Saint Anthony Abbot,

Saints Polycarp and Chrysostom and Aquinas,
pages from one of our eleven thousand tomes

touching from the serpent to the horses
of the Apocalypse. Always at my back I sensed

the old scribes with their pigments, the elaborate
whorls of their visions, but for me there was only

the next-to-silent scritching of a pen; under high
and narrow windows, radiators ticked, and I thought

of those saints, with the self-swallowing, fabulous
animals of their lettering, their blaeberry wimberry

texturings, who welcomed penances in their cells,
self-flagellation, their fingers hooked, the crozier-

crook of their spines over their cold
library of seven books. Soon I would walk –

the *liber usualis* in my hand – down narrow corridors,
keeping always, in humility, close against the walls,

eyes in custody, to sing out vespers, compline,
relishing the long, hushed centuries of the plainsong,

anticipating the comforts of a silent, and a long, night:
in manus tuas Domine commendo spiritum meum.

The Pride of Life

for Tim Sheehan

McGarvey and I were young and male and speaking
of the concupiscence of eyes, of flesh,
of the pride of life; our God, old Taskmaster,
demanded of us perfection, suffering and Latin.

McGarvey and I were dressing boards
of flesh-coloured deal, dovetailing them
into library shelves when the chisel,
curved like the quarter moon, slipped, and sliced

into my index finger; maladroit, I watched
blood spurt until the pain scalded me
and I sat down, stunned, amongst wood-shavings
and white dust; *in illo tempore* seminarians,

McGarvey and I (like Christ himself) were in otherwhere
on carpentry assignment, though I was more
for the study of Aquinas and the Four Last Things, more
apt with pen and paper and the ancient texts;

my finger-flesh had lifted and I tied it, tight,
with my seminarian's white handkerchief – *you're
pale as a ghost*, McGarvey said, that ghost
still with me now, pen in hand, wandering the world,

a fine-curved scar on my index finger;
a solitary gladiolus, elegant and tall,
of a cardinal brightness, beckons to me
from outside the window, and that young seminarian –

misfit and eager, trenchant and melancholy
in the pursuit of love – haunts me still, his God
and McGarvey's God, displaced, replaced, my God
untonsured now, and feminine, and here.

The Rose Window

A sparrow flew, as if a hawk were in pursuit,
into the sanctuary of our seminary chapel;
I was quenching candles, relishing the afterscent;

it perched a while on a small brass crucifix
over the tabernacle, and I remembered: *better are you*
than many sparrows, and laughed, not being sure... I stood,

hesitant companion, the congregation with its shuffle-noise
had gone out into the good air; for a while –
acolyte and bird – we watched each other, intrigued

and waiting; the sparrow flew towards the rose window
where it thudded hard against deceptive blue; it fell,
slowly, to the marble floor and I gathered it up, scared,

knowing, for a moment, what it may be to be God,
a small heart hammering against my caring hands; outside
sweet scents from the heathers came and clouds drifted

across blue late-evening skies; when I opened my hands
the sparrow stayed still a little while, perhaps
mistrusting of the grace it had just received.

Leftovers

The old man, out and almost-down, reeks
of dank doorways, of unwashed clothes; sits

by the church steps, a Styrofoam crushed mug
held up for coins; he sees us, indistinctly, shades

garnering small graces at his expense; hurt heron,
will sleep tonight in a cardboard refrigerator-box

withstanding weather better than we do. Here,
underneath the layers of dirt and shabbiness

there is vulnerable flesh, its valleys, its portals
sacred as our own. Behind the blank though watchful

eyes, beyond the scars and stubble and beneath
the matted heron-grey topknot of his hair

there is a mind as friable as ours, and a soul
sought for by the wandering, the forlorn Christ –

heron, God's loved leftover bird, slow to lift
out of muddied waters into a doubtful sky.

Before the Crib

Unprecedented warmth had kept the herd
out in the fields till Advent; I saw their breathing, mornings,
hover over them like a cloud; later I could hear

snuffling and jostling in the slatted shed, cumbersome
flesh confined, the occasional clang of iron like a deadened
bell ringing. Christmas, I knelt before the crib to see

the ox, watchful over the newly born who held, already,
both hands high in blessing; straw leaked from the patched roof,
Joseph stood, bland and painted, one arm broken off

at the elbow; I sniffed for the stench of cattle in cramped
spaces, finding it difficult to hold belief that here
is God's handiwork, here eternity has crawled into restricted

times and places, closing the distances between divinity
and dearth, between the heavens and the run-down church;
I wanted everything to change, I was a child, longing,

but without the words to plead. Now I pray, out
of the tragedy that is the history of our endeavour, to find
eternity in the bones of time, malice and greed subsumed

in the outspread hands of the Christ, pray for faithfulness
beyond all guile, that we who are made of a yielding clay
may be, in deed, far more than we imagine.

A Birth

Yeshua, at your birth, did the angels
sing Vivaldi's *Gloria*? and the shepherds,
did they play jaws harp, Jews' harp, tonguing
Dvořák's *New World Symphony*? The spheres –
were they humming, as twilight turned
from tangerine to emerald, and down
to a drear and turquoise basso – did the stars
sound out Bruckner, Brahms and Bach?
That sheep may safely graze… Or was it merely
the snuffling of animals in their stalls, dawn-music
played each morning in the small farms, the opening
of stable doors, or city-sounds of preparation
for another day, like an orchestra tuning up, this
puer natus, this image of love, of God invisible.

Butcher

I heard the tick-tick-tick of his bicycle
as he pushed into the yard, then his loud halloo –
MEAT. The Sunday joint was wrapped in newspaper,

blood on the pages, blood on the twine, blood soon
on the notes mother handed over. Sometimes a misty rain
sent small pink drops onto the road, like a trail,

from the wicker basket over the front wheel.
He set his butcher's workshop on a green space
out in the bogland; on hooks, by the whitewashed wall,

sheep carcases hung, the Atlantic winds shifting them
like slowest pendulums. I was sent across to collect
the Christmas turkey; I remember raindrops

gathered in winter sunshine and glistening on wire fencing,
delicate as the shivering tinsel on our tree. I heard the dull
thud of a chopping knife, saw the hacked wood of the block

and the slow dribble-drip of black blood down the timber.
He mocked me, the butcher, his big face round and florid,
his butcher's apron stained and streaked. At midnight

when I knelt a while before the caverned crib, I could find
no words; you were there, in the glow of candlelight, straw
holding you, your pale hands raised towards me, welcoming.

Name and Nature

Your name, Jesus, is childhood in the body, at times
a single malt upon the tongue, Vivaldi to the ears;

your name, Christ, forgiveness to the heart, acceptance
to the flesh, a troubled joy across the soul;

at ever my very best I will plead to you, closest to me,
for kindness. Perhaps the silence I take for God's

non-presence is the noise in which I have immersed
my life; nor have I framed a quiet to correspond

to His, where I might find my every call
answered. I seek kind. You are the reality I cling to,

the flesh, the history, the spurting out of blood. I believe
the non-attendance of my God lies in my absence from Him

and He is present, like the embrace of air
or the inward forces of the seasons. Your name, Jesus,

is the river on which I float, your name, Christ, the ocean
where everything is in place, is shivering, beautiful, and apart.

Late in the Season

The first dense fog this morning, everything
indistinct. Small birds

flit among stones at the waves' edge; last night
along laneways and in the meadows,

heavy tractors laboured on, their headlights flaring;
among the sand dunes rabbits

played with cloudshadows from the moon; now a fox
in her potched, gold–chestnut fur

scents out her lost escape-ways through the lopped–down grass.
I have been picturing

a straight and solitary figure pacing the roads and shoreline
as if washed up onto the world

like jetsam flung by the breaking reach of the waves,
who has words to offer, words

in an antique language beautiful as moonlight and sharp
as the teeth of the mowers,

while the world feels for him, offering
unwanted coin.

Clew Bay, 1894, 2010

for James Harpur

The sacred mountain rose
        into untarnished light, its summit
        haloed with snow, and all the islands
        sailed on the bay in soft-pink morning glory;

a solitary swan, like a flake
        off the mountain-top, came
        flying in over the marshes, intent and
        slow as grief, its plumage sullied; it circled

low over the estuary
        then laboured off towards distant trees;
        there was, riding the air, a sense of loss,
        of long disquiet, and of uncertain homing.

For every reason, and for none,
        I thought of the Achill hooker –
        its cargo of souls intent and brooding
        towards the tattie fields of Scotland – that day

it sank in the swell off Westport,
        sent thirty-two young emigrants
        into God's cold bosom. High tide now
        washes against kelp-darkened walls, a rusted spar

scrapes lazily against abandoned
        fish-factory sheds, mud-bubbles lift
        to the untroubled surface of the sea; Clew Bay,
        home-scape of myths and seasons, its many islands

ruminating like sea-cows
        on sweet meadows of the ocean,
        how the world's grandeur is like stained
        down, how sorrow comes homing in on a sea-breeze

while the heart is circling
in ever-more-demanding need
for a certain landing-place; dawn lightening
into another day, an austere ancestry brooding over all.

Nocturne

for Eva Bourke

Dark night comes slowly, a black-wool blanket
    drawn up across the sky, moth-holes you may see
    clean through to the original source of light;
    there is, as always, a little night-music:

the vesper-hymn of jasmine, compline of night-
    scented stock – *Salve Regina*, and *Nunc Dimittis*...
    Just once, thunder grumbles at a great distance;
    for hours, moonlight touches so lightly

on the white keys of the piano you cannot hear the so-slow
    rising of the scale (C major, legato, no sharps, no flats);
    blackthorn bushes in their shrouds of white
    stir abroad, like familial, kindly ghosts

who tell us they are angels now, can no more die;
    softly they speak together, young children
    of the resurrection, peaceful through the reaches
    of eternity; and if, they say, tomorrow, you are graced again

to lift your faces to the risen sun, do not yet
    envy us, citizens long past night; relish, they say,
    the munificence of primroses along the ditch and the thought
    of ruby-coloured sloe gin at this year's end.

Reasons of the Heart

for Paddy Bushe

Reason dictates one does not build a monastery
      on a desolate high rock miles out to sea; reason
      knows it as a soaring-place for fulmar, a burrow-home
      for the tubenose shearwater; and yet –

should you stand, one night, when the sea
      breathes quietly below, when the sky has grown
      close and spectacular in its stars, should you watch
      this day's companion climb, crisscross upwards through the dark

with only the shifting light of his storm-lantern telling
      his passageway to the heavens – then you will know
      you are safe here, out of the world's wildering. The soul
      thrives in compulsive prayers and praisings;

so climb, pilgrim, to heights that take the breath away
      until you stand at last, head in the clouds, undaunted.
      To carve, over years-or-life, rough cruciform shapes
      out of the livid rock may be a poem to what reason calls

foolishness: word made stone, made bone, clay-floor
      and weathers. Here you may miss the galloping of horses
      over sward, but you are rid of newspapers, banks
      and metaphysical concerns. Perhaps, who knows? the Christ

shifts stealthily about the slopes, freed from reason's grounds,
      here where seals come, heaving themselves onto rock
      to flop and doze, their deep-voiced moaning songs
      calling out crazed praise to their Creator.

Muir Woods, California

22 October 2010

Redwoods, sequoia sempervirens, steeple-tall,
where we walked, awed to silence, through a past
present to us in the trees, centuries old,
the soft rain's sibilance holding all the woods
in an embrace of stillness; down the rich aisles
of pillared trees that soared, reaching high
as old God's leaning, we found ourselves
insignificant, temporal beings, taken by the impulse
to pray; till we saw the owl, squat on a branch,
watchful Methuselah, barred owl, old hinge-head,
swivel-face and rain-owl, bemused at us who mooched
by below, uncertain, turning to our cellphones
for assurance, our cars waiting in the carpark,
urgent for the forecourts, the switchbacks, the freeways;
you could hear them, the redwoods, in the mists
gossiping about the restlessness of humankind,
who, for the moment, struggle with our illnesses,
with the loveliness of the roe-deer skittering
across our path, elegant and fearful, and the buck
quick in his balletic leap into the ferns till we know
we have dipped our fingers in a sacred font
and emerge, fortified by sacrament, blessed again in spirit
for our ongoing struggle with the flesh.

Bunnacurry Pier

i.m. Declan Deane 1942–2010

It was morning then in the world, and we –
acolytes together – sang to the God who gave joy
to our youth. It is morning yet, in the still
backward of the soul that is memory, holding firm

across rise and ebb of happiness and grief. We ran
down to the pier, with makeshift rods, makeshift
lines and hooks, the waters of Blacksod Bay
brimming; we would be fishermen, we would be

fabulous, for the juvenile pollack came, *bullagógs*,
plumped to a silvering dark-green shape, big
as our father's thumb, flickering in the dark-green
tide; we caught them, baiting hooks with the drawn-out

flesh of periwinkles, hoisting the tiddlers proudly up
to the rough-stone pier. We were raucous together then,
content – for now – in the slow upwelling of our lives
and beyond us, out there, the continents, the tides,

the harbours. And now, after it all, the decades, the deaths,
does the heart still sing? Remember how the story-teller
asked: what are you afraid of? Don't you know that
once upon a time, Christ himself, our Little Father, died?

Brother

*in memoriam Rev. Declan Deane, born Achill Island 14 May 1942,
died Pleasant Hill, California 12 December 2010*

Nunc, et in perpetuum, frater, ave atque vale

After the funeral Mass, concelebrating priests
filed out behind the casket, in white surplices
and black soutanes, like a fleet of small boats

leaving harbour under sail; they gathered
in late-morning sunshine to sing –
while dark-suited men lifted you carefully

into the hearse – the Latin hymn of our exile: *Salve
Regina;* male voices, a medieval chant, carried on the breeze
but all I saw was the dizzying flight of a humming-bird,

emerald with breast of scarlet, at the higher branches
of a tree, salutary, like an amen, like a reassurance
from the world; *vita, dulcedo, et spes nostra, salve...*

★

Brother. Belovèd. I have been following...
On the way to school, remember, I
loitering; on the way home, scuffing
grasses by the roadside, or flinging stones

at high, unreachable gulls. Remember, evenings,
Bunnacurry, Achill Island, Co. Mayo,
how we stood together at the grove's edge,
stilled by the song of the blackbird, flute-rich

and visceral, *In the beginning...* And follow still,
though I found you exhausted by that dread
and body-gnawing illness, and I felt shy of you,
we two, brothers, reaching out to one another

99

for comfort. In Pleasant Hill, breezes touch the leaves
into wind-song, while soul so clings to body
it is a passionate love affair, and will not last.
On the Golden Strand, remember? playmates

we built our moats and castles, learned to swim
in the easy waves of Blacksod Bay, stood
on jagged rocks at ocean's edge and watched out
over the vast uncertain, children, open, awed.

★

We sat, again together, in your room,
the small gatherings of a lifetime, photos, books,
in an ordered disarray; and spoke of death, of faith…

and you were famine-famished, broken; you spoke
the hymn you loved, your voice still firm
and I knew you had left me far behind,

struggling still, beloved brother, for reassurance:
Abide with me, fast falls the eventide;
The darkness deepens, Lord with me abide;

you tried the melody, but your voice broke:
Change and decay in all around I see;
O Thou who changest not, abide with me.

★

God surrounds, the way the universe surrounds,
impels, as the universe impels – seasons,
fall and spring, cancer, volcano, song;
and there you were, too soon, almost prostrate

though I believe your Christ, eyes bright with gladness,
was visible to you, there, just out beyond
the eucalyptus, your awkward, demanding, loved
Jesus, companion in the dread, the laughter.

Before *Iliad* and *Odyssey*, remember?
how big the meadows by the old house, how huge
the haycocks that we conquered, how powerful the weapons,
the wooden rake, the hayfork; speak to me now

how the world shrinks, how progress and neglect
make a wilderness, hiding the luscious honey-nests
of the distraught humble-bee, blotting out
two grinning boys, two innocents who stood

naked to the waist and red with sun. Evening
and I was walking with you round the parking lot,
Christ the King Parish, diocese of Oakland, California:
the cancer raddling you, slowing you to a soft-

shoe shuffle, you (this once) following, but the Christ, too,
walked with us, offering you the grace of suffering
while I stumbled, bewildered ever, incapable. Love
is a demanding fugue across our days, notes

of a rendered music building always
to a *Totenlied*. You moved now, as Mary moved,
smitten by knowledge, setting out over the most
barren of landscapes, in expectation.

★

And here I am again, following, though most
unwilling. Schoolchildren line the road, the broad
Gregory Lane, Pleasant Hill, California, their hands
raised to you in blessing and farewell. Tears in the eyes

of many children. Tears in mine. The quiet hearse
moves slowly, sunlight gleaming on its chrome, its polished
mirroring black. I in the next car, following. Scent of eucalyptus
heavy on the air. You and I, Declan, children together, remember?

All of us children, *exules, filii Evae. Ad te clamamus...*
I had rehearsed your dying, wondering at times
if this is dream or nightmare, everything coming apart
as cloud-wisps do, seen through the small window

101

of a plane, that fear when turbulence unsettles you,
and your fingers grip – in involuntary dread – the hard
seat-rests and you look for destination, the old
sense of belonging when you stride out boldly

towards arrival hall, reassured once more, on good ground.
And then we stood, sodden with our grieving, as you
went down, too young, out of the light, leaving us
to bear the unacceptable burden of your dying,

nothing between me and the dark, now you are gone.
And Brian Joyce, speaking the prayers out loud,
sending a sprinkling of water, like love-tears, towards you.
I dropped some red and golden roses down with you, tokens

of our incapacity with words. Perhaps ours is the dream
of blackbird, singing out of dusk, offering us all
the coming-together again, for the last time, of the light
and night. *Ad te clamamus, ad te clamamus.*

Unfinished Symphony

The berries on the holly tree are vivid red;
it is late in the year, the world spread out
in manuscript of black and grey and white,

branches bared like staves, waiting. This is Ireland,
the music has been cacophonous, Church
and state and weathers. Someone, in the island chapel,

was practising the harmonium when I came in,
dark afternoon, the pews deserted; I listened,
it was an Advent hymn – *Puer natus in Bethlehem* –

anticipating. Outside again, I watched two hares
go bounding over the shorn meadow, blackberries
have plumped into scintillating black, the bramleys

have been harvested from the tree by the red gate
and all the earth, this while, is rife again
with the part-notated manuscript of a symphony,

clef and key-signature, and every possibility.
Tonight I was gazing up through the glass roof
of the sunroom, a gang of daws passed hurriedly

towards the wood and a barn owl, magnificent
in its gentlemanly flight, went by. Here is the long struggle
towards the harmonies, there are the false notes,

the wrong keys; the heart lifts, after all, to the starlight
and are you not amazed, father, mother, brother, anticipating
that great finale, *incarnatus est*, that thunderous Amen!

VII

Blessed and Broken: A Sequence

Note

Names of people and places in the New Testament are used in this sequence according to the way the originals are translated by Willis Barnstone in *The Restored New Testament*, New York, W.W. Norton & Co. Ltd, 2009.

Abram:	Abraham
ben-Yosef:	son of Joseph
Galil:	Galilee
Gat-Shmanim:	Gethsemane: Oil-Press
Ha-Maschiach:	The Messiah
Kfar Nahum:	Capernaum
Loukas:	Luke
Magdil:	Magdala
Markos:	Mark
Mattityahu:	Matthew
Miryam:	Mary
Miryam of Magdil:	Mary Magdalene
Moshe:	Moses
Shlomo:	Solomon
Yarden:	the river Jordan
Yermiyahu:	Jeremiah
Yerushalayim:	Jerusalem
Yeshua:	Jesus
Yohanan:	John

Blessed and Broken

The Lord bless you and keep you.
The Lord make his face to shine upon you
and be gracious to you;
The Lord turn his face towards you and give you peace

(Numbers 6: 24–26)

I

The Lake

Flight

Lufthansa, to Frankfurt, to Tel Aviv. Night-flight,
the relief of a good book and a glass of garnet-red

wine that shades to black in the deep of the glass.
Introductions all round: the firm grip, at times

the already withdrawing grasp – Fellow Pilgrims!
Terminal, time for a coffee, a short perhaps, perhaps

a Danish. Grey evening, good for flying.
And what are you going out into the world to see?

exotica, date-palms, a hot-wind shore: where two
or fifty-three are gathered together in his name...

wonders of the flesh and spirit, a road-map for a shattered
faith. We, for a time, to be sojourners in a foreign land :

The Golan Heights

We have crossed the trickle of Yarden, river
of myth and mystery, before turning up
towards the heights, skirting borders, their reaching

electrified wires, their laid-down mines. There is a long
sweeping, upward-curving road
out of Tiberias, where breath hangs out over chasms

and our bus goes labouring up, capable any moment
of precipitation into Jordan valleys. Alpha ghosts
of past wars and invasions, inhabit the zee-curves

and abandoned bunkers, and hot winds sweep across
from Syria. The Golan Heights watch out over the Galil
as great-great-grandpa God must watch, sipping the best vintage

through the changeless dusk that is eternity. Far below
the lake of miracles, of unexpected storms;
in the distance Hermon stands

in its dressing-gown of snow. Suddenly
Israeli murder-jets fly past in earth-juddering noise and anger,
till all I can think of are the naked feet of Christ

passing slowly over the pebbled dust of the Galil
in search of some
who will take up love by the cupful

and swallow it down whole :

Angel Wings

I see you, Yeshua, step out of the fishing-boat
into shallow water; you are being driven on

by your demons; naked, your feet are bruised
by lake-shore shells, *angel wings, periwinkle,*

limpet, clam; I see, and do not see, you
glance up towards the lush hills of the Gadarenes,

the junipers, the cyclamens, the hyacinths, while high above
a honey buzzard soars on the breadth of air.

Tale of the daimon within, spirit within the spirit,
body within the body's frame, goading, and constraining;

what I search for in you is mercy. The mountain's flank
is scored with caves, and the Wildman comes screaming down –

the suffering greater than body or soul can entertain –
image of humankind in dark estrangement from itself.

I see us, too, in our newer generations, for we are legion,
chained and breaking free, in need (in spite

of our loudest selves) of you, touch, words, or gaze.
A flock of pelicans has lifted heavily into sky; I look out

for you, a small boat coming in towards shore, you watch
upwards, mercy a blue stone in the dark of your eyes :

The Predator

Mornings, when I plead for care across the day,
the image of you, Yeshua Ha-Maschiach,
walking by the shores of the great lake

disturbs me; those were not sophisticated men
but something in their living – at the edge of waters, dependent –
lay vulnerable to your summoning words. I see you

predator, hovering: beak and claws, wings and talons,
an exacting love. I am restless always
with distracting questions, disturbances persisting,

I labour to let you in. We are suffering the consequences
of greed, like an Irish winter, days opening to a long barrage of rain,
unmanning desperation in the souls of many; and what

is left to us? Yeshua, you, while blackbird and long-tailed tit
still come scattering across the gardens with their songs
and tsirrupings, how they weave and float and flit,

giving momentary respite :

The Inland Sea

This is the lake, Tiberias, its sea-waters,
I dreamed it often in my deep-night watches,
to take it to my soul that I might own it.

Imagine! running at speed across the surface,
elated at salvation; and though I set aside raw moments
that I may pray, the static of the universe

intrudes; I search the stillness that is beyond words
for the one Word. Winds are fickle as my faith;
here reeds and sedge and warblers, boardwalk,

souvenir and pilgrim-babble. Out of the hills the lightning,
sudden as the word *Christ* shattering the gloom, like glass,
casting ghost-light over lake and boat; thunder-blast

and the flinging up of spray against the boat
like swarms of bees and hornets with a will to batter us
out of all complaisance. We huddle down

behind umbrellas, wind-cheaters, with our phones and cameras,
praying you will be there, after all this, while spirit stirs
on deep, engrossing waters, in the wolfstorm dark, in the watches

of the day, that you still our fears, that you quieten
our appetites, that you reach out to us in our drowning,
scared you might abandon us where we call,

certain, uncertain, you might stride on by :

Encounter

It is March; in Ireland
daffodils will be suffering the harshest winds; here
the coach had turned back from the slopes of the Beatitudes
towards Tiberias; to the right

the valleys, green and flush,
rising to the hills; to the left, the lake, quietened
in an evening lull and pleasuring.
I settled in my seat, comforted, and tired; when –

and this is my wakeful dream, the happening, the real –
in the coach-seats opposite, father,
fisherman and March-month birthday-boy,
and brother, Declan,

impatient God-lover, picketer by the gates
of San Quentin, celebrant of falling free at last
from alcohol addiction: both of them
in animated conversation, both of them dead

for years, and months; they spoke
in a language without words, song-like, seductive.
Outside, darkness was falling early, the sun
a dying fire, light catching

on the thorn of the moon that was lying idle
in a sapphire-shaded heaven; soon there would be shimmering
silver nightways out across the sea. Father
suddenly called to me, and pointed; the bus

stopped, and we stepped down, we three, only;
silently they walked across the grass, down
towards the shore;
drawn, confused, I followed,

the light so faint now all was shadow,
father, old friend, and faithful; Declan, brother, and priest.
The old man turned to me, and smiled, 'we,' he said, 'we
are not in death, we are in life.'

He pointed. There was another
standing near the lake, her back to us, she was watching
out over the water, frail-boned, slight
but firm. 'Mother?' I said and she turned,

slowly; I did not know her; fair-skinned,
handsome but not beautiful. 'Your name?' I asked;
'Miryam,' she said, 'Miryam of Magdil. And yours?'
'Yohanan,' I answered, to my surprise. Around us

ruins only, excavations, stone-heaps, stumps – Magdil?
'It was here,' she said, 'he
stepped ashore from the fishing-boat;
and stood awhile, gazing towards the hills; I

was kneeling, there, by that great rock;
I was gutting fish, for salting; I worried for his feet,
naked against the sharp edges of the shells;
the others, fishermen, moved awkwardly,

hauling the boat ashore, uncertain of themselves;
and "who are you?" I asked him
though I already knew the answer; he
is the way, he is the life, and his truth

will sear both soul and body. And he said, "Miryam",
as if he knew me; "if I give," he said,
"word of myself, what can that be to you? Come,
and see." And I left fish, and shore, lake and village

and followed him. He is invasion, hero, mystery,
he is the centre, he is forgiveness, light. And now I,' she said,
'am in death no longer, I am in life.' She smiled,
turning back towards the sea;

I glanced for father, brother, but they were
not there and when I turned again, she, too, had disappeared.
I shivered suddenly, alone, and cold; a black-backed gull,
perched on the great rock,

was stabbing down
at some small feathered thing.
Now it was night;
from the road Abram was calling out to me

and I came back, at peace, heavy in flesh, but free :

Just a Closer Walk with Thee

At the foot of the hill of transfiguration
the taxi-cabs, the shops, the souvenirs;

the zig-zag climb, mimosa, date palms, scrub,
always anticipation, then the mild let-down;

the church, the crowds above, as it was, as is,
as it will be, and you, Yeshua, beloved, amongst us

somewhere in the crush, the sacrament, the dream.
Chill winds were blowing up from the Galil, we

wrapped in ourselves, and the Japanese with their covenants
of cameras and phones. Tired,

a little disappointed, I stood apart, watching out
from the high wall; buzzards were black blots

thermal-hugging against the sky, nearby a sparrow –
busy as ever in the brush and dust – held herself

in the Father's eye. And there it was, far below me,
the small town – Nain – off to the south-east, like a mirage

in near-desert heat beyond; and all the years I have lived
flooded me, like wine, so that all now I could see

was figures in a landscape, out of Rembrandt or Van Gogh,
light battering the darkness to touch on death

with an overarched respect. An old-time funeral, something like
New Orleans, for instance, flowed out of the town, the music

echoing up to me from the plain, horns and timbrel, shofar, flute,
dirge and wailing, drifting into jazz, *just a closer walk*

with Thee, as you, Yeshua, came walking slowly, a few
wreck-ribbed curs nearby rooting in the dust; and always

the widow's son, father, mother, brother, wife… I expected,
up here on the hill, the heavy tolling of a bell: that solitary

brass-hasped heart-beat, remembering small towns in the far west,
Foxford, Balla, the deathsome rites, *dies irae, dies illa*, the hopeless

drawing-down of curtains as the cortège passed, the hearse,
that weight of grief until 'Enough!' the poet said,

'the Resurrection!' and You, Yeshua, blessed and broken
are walking still, slowly towards the edge of town,

towards Foxford, Balla, Haifa, Nagasaki, Rome :

Reed-Music

Spring; the breeze has still a blade
      edge, the air a gentian blue caress;
there are lambs in the fields of Tabgha,
      snow on the shoulders of Hermon;

we stood awhile on the lush
      slopes of the Beatitudes, hearts
buoyant in the morning light; blessed
      are they who are loved, and those who love

are blessed. There came to mind
      a hill beyond Dooagh, how the rogue dogs –
where the furze was in golden-chalice bloom –
      savaged a scattering of lambs and left

blood-pall on the baby-wool, limbs
      torn, and that feeble, plaintive crying
that takes you by the heart.
      Here, at lake's edge, there is reed-music,

warblers clinging with thread-thin claws
      the way our faith clings and will not be broken
by any unholy wind. Then, the light
      dawning, the fishermen saw a presence

on the rock: 'Who is he?' they whispered, scared
      they might already know. Now,
on this rock – this one, as well as any other –
      candles are offering a small

surf of tears, weeping as they die, in the mere
      possibility of joy. We stood by the lakeshore,
in the watermusic of a presence, the heartstrings
      plucked, the irregular pulsebeat

of the waves, bone-hymns of the shore, amongst billions
        of tiny pastel-coloured shells. We heard
the Christ-questions in our world of hurt: *do you*
        love me? and how they rushed to land, *but do you love*

me? a fire already lit, fish broiling: *I ask you, do*
        you love me?, showing them the livid
blood-pall bruises… *feed my sheep* – and I know how much
        needs to be said, and how words stream away,

        blue ink, into the blue waters of the sea :

Capernaum

He came here, too, to Kfar Nahum, moving
in the likeness of sinful flesh, intruder, a stumbling block,

setting up house amongst those living streets,
neighbour, importunate for love;

these are the windings of my days, too, these
the destructive winds, the black

stumps of all my doubts; body and spirit suffering
difficult cohabitation, dreading ruin.

On the shores of the lake we stood a while,
the yeshua-yeshua hushing of our griefs

coming in towards us across the shingles,
as if, somehow, everything may yet not be lost.

Village of Nahum, stands now
like a dusk-lit city of gravestones;

these were streets, like ours, like mine,
donkey-hooves on cobbles, a haggle-babble

bustle of human flesh in the busyness of barter,
fish-market, fish-wives, fish-guts; there were roofs

thatched with palm-leaves friable as straw,
gutters, thresholds, homes

and the backyard warmth of cockerel and hen;
and he walked here, to whom my soul clings,

offering love like home-made ware too easily
flung back at him and smashed; God-Man, Man-God,

the offence, rejected, risen, the scandalon; ever
present to us now who will lie, at times,

prone on the pallets of ourselves, longing –
scared – to be laid at the feet of this persistent lover :

The Poem

By stepping down into the poem I can meet
      with her, dead now
for as many years as I am living. See her, with the family,
there in the side aisle, in churchday best,

and me, days-old boy scarce dried from the warm waters
      of the womb.
Listen! it's Father Tiernan, murmuring; and that sudden
brass-and-polished-wood and hollow-echoing sound is the door

banging shut in a draught;
      (me, too,
making my presence felt at my christening nigh
seventy years ago); it is my Christ-

ening, in white cotton gown, white woollen shawl, and Patricia
      holding me in her arms

while Father Tiernan importantly
says a blessing on the water. She was beautiful,

that much they told me, later
          (and can see it for myself,
now) a 1940s beauty, the fine lips redly pouting, the sculpted
eyebrows, the tailored suit,

that war-time curling hair up-do; godmother, aunt
          too young and lovely
to be crucified by TB. And me, ignorant, innocent, unknowing,
where does it all leave me?

here, by Yarden river, standing in the flow beneath
the whispering eucalyptus.
                    We, the pilgrims,
have stepped down again out of our comfort

to be close to the river's source, by the fern-green sluggish flow
and shallow curve, willing wayfarers
                    keen to dip themselves –
white gowns, white sneakers, dozens of them now, holding hands,

up to their breasts in the stream –
Malaysian, Australian, Greek – immersing all together and holding:
                    one – two – three, and up
to hymns and hallelujahs,

shaking Yarden water out of hair and eyes.
An egret, white as a ghost, flies low over the water, upstream,
          making for the lake; on the further bank
the umbels of the hemlock are a white haze, the pilgrims' hymns

are shaded many languages, and the waters flowing down
          carry off
cargoes of sin, and darkness, down to the tideless sea.
I sit awhile, bemused; Patricia

speaks my name aloud, Yohanan, she says, Yohanan,
          the soft grey of her eyes

lit with a gentling light, the end
and the beginning holding hands in unconscious hope;

and I
have been here before, as if to touch the Yarden waters
will bring me close to her, bring her back to me, godmother, urging
the life of Christ. It's a question

of trying to save us
from war, from – let me write the word down – from
evil; question of being held by those who love us
over, and into, the water; to place us in the flow with the purer spirits,

so that, said Yeshua ben-Yosef,
they may all be one as we, Father, are one,
I in them and You in me, that they be made perfect in one.
Meaning, the nations

designing treaties amongst themselves and with themselves,
uttering that one word mercy meaning
love meaning Yeshua the Mashiach the One immersed
here at the head of the waters:

and just like stepping down into the flow of the Yarden now,
I step
down into the poem, taking with me the spirits
of those present, future, past, the dead, the friends, the foes,

the blessed, the broken, Jaffa, Nablus, Dublin, Derry,
the crossroads, bullets, bombs,
taking them all in my arms, here, within the poem, within the flow,
and praying – please, still it may be possible – still.

And then, and now, Patricia kisses me, a kiss
soft as a touch out of Genesis,
there by the brawn marble base, the white marble font,
the water poured, and here, by the river's flow

she says my name, aloud: Yohanan, she says, Yohanan
and I close, quietly, the chapel door

and take my place once more, here, ageing, and still
a pilgrim, in prayer by Yarden shore :

Mount Hermon

And then we moved aside a while, outside
pilgrimage, to sit at table on the lakeshore terraces,
four or five gathered together, a presence amongst us
greater than our individual presences. The sun

was going down, behind the city of Tiberias,
touching the Galil with fluid colours, and snow-bound Hermon
shifting from softest pink to rose, into a shimmering
soft-toned emerald, then shading down to grey. Israeli

war-jets flew shuddering the air over the lake, high
aggressive pterodactyls utterly out of place. We said the name,
Yeshua, Yeshua, shared wine and breads and oil, spoke of him

in sacrament and sharing. Word. Entire. Yeshua calling us
by name. I spoke a psalm, language but no words, within me. Ah well:

we are witnesses to wonders, and we have news to tell :

II

To the City

Route 90

We are taking the coach south now, route 90, out of Tiberias;
through Yarden valley, the plush, dark-green exuberance of the Galil;

comfortable pilgrims, breakfasted, our prayers and morning hymns
cushions to our progress; *Christ be with me, Christ before...*

The eucalyptus, the Judas tree, the olive tree, the cypress,
awkward banana groves, oranges, lemons, figs...

ancient tombs and easy-minded small and half-forgotten synagogues,
the small-town well-being, the world so strange and so familiar...

We pass with such goodly nonchalance as we can muster, on the
                                                    long road
up to Yerushalayim. To the left the Jordan border, double line

of electrified fencing, keeping fear out, holding it in;
on the dirt road alongside, an Israeli Storm jeep, machine-gun

nests atop, guns primed and pointing... dust, coloured rust and blood,
rising behind in a stormcloud. This land brings the dead to mind,
                                                    as if they

straggled here, unsettled amongst the living; or perhaps it is the living
who straggle, unsettled, amongst the dead; Yeshua, too, silent and grim,

is straggling here, unsettled, forever on the road up to Yerushalayim :

Qumran

Here, on the hard-baked earth of Palestine, teach me how
to pray, to kneel, eyes shut, or stand, turning towards the naked hills
of Qumran, touching the baked earth, feeling the heat. The spirit

droops, arid as the desert, crushed by silence, sometimes doubt,
while the ravening scream of a raptor, in the searing sky, shakes me,
with the speaking emptiness of the excavations, the dust-filled cisterns

till I fall aware of distances, from home, and self, and You; Yeshua,
alpha, omega, anointed and humiliated, hidden focus and still
point of history, past and future, who burn the heart in the futility

of this ungraspable moment, *now*. I walk about the site, ropes guiding;
is this prayer? does it reach You? where the hills retain the sheltering
darkness of the caves, a barrenness that breeds scorpions, perhaps,

locusts, honey, the half-crazed rant of driven saints, as if you could fish
in rock, and hook a scroll that would clarify it all, Your name and
nature,
my name and nature... till I seek relief in the distracting, familiar truth

of the souvenir shop, in guava juices and the sweet and bitter
grapefruit :

The Bedouin

The West Bank, Palestine occupied. To the right
the beginnings of desert, scrub, loose stones on the low slopes,

rock dunes, erratics, the colours fading from kaleidoscope
to uniform ochre. Wayfarers still, we sit, entranced; glimpses

from the coach, of Bedouin, an old man astride a donkey,
flocks of goats following; further off, along a gulley, tents

in disarray, a camel standing, dull as rock; honey-coloured
gathering hills, all naked boulder, and how can it sustain

122

mind or body? Samaria, its own graceland, struggle of the spirit
for reason, faith, survival – and we, complacent in our bus,

cruise on by, for now, the unknown Yeshua stalking us,
dark-skinned, dour, impoverished, on the edge...

We turn off a while, a coffee-break, a small
oasis. Out on Route 90, articulated trucks speed past,

coach, and car and caravan, the human restlessness
intent upon its fevers; there is a shack, cheap goods, a parched

olive tree growing up through an abandoned car, a few
rib-rabble dogs cautious by the galvanised latrine – but the coffee

is good, the sesame breads, and a stuttering old-world radio
plays harsh unrecognised music. I stand aside a moment, back

at our island crossroads, late-40s Ireland, harshness
our mode and being, an unrefined old testament Jehovah

frowning down in rain and darkness – till I hear again the heart-cry
for our redemption, how one much greater than we are, urgent

with care, must come to save us – and know that I should kneel,
here, under the sun, touching the edge of the impossible; but I, too,

have grown sophisticate and modern, citizen of the blessed and broken
first world, and so I speak my plea in quiet, in the cold irrational
place within

where I may pray. Out on Route 90, there are shapes in the
heat-shimmer
off the asphalt, ghosts at play, sweeping themselves in the wake

of trucks and cars, perpetual hastening, something to be discovered,
somewhere else, not here, not here... And soon the coach will turn,

at last, onto Route 1, climbing to Yerushalayim, while we fall silent,
pleading, without words, frightened now of what we may not find... :

Walls

I stand – a continent away
from the crumbled walls of Bunnacurry two-room school –
now, at last, by the Western Wall,
leaning my hands against its massive stones, and seeking words;

'in Yerushalayim,' the Spirit wrote, 'shall be my name forever';

to my left, black coat and pants,
white shirt and thick grey beard, kippah, prayer shawl, a man
sways back and forth in prayer –
hear, O Yisrael, The Lord our God, the Lord is one... Torah, psalms;

our little catechism asked: *does God*

know all things? The high partition
between the rooms squealed on its castors, folding open,
when Father Tiernan came
to test our souls; *God knows all things, even*

our most secret thoughts and actions. I relished then

the loveliness of the near-rhymes,
the old-fashioned *doth*-and-*dost* of the English, leaving
a softly-furred coating on the soul. I need to know
the rough texture of a wall you could break your life against; and so

I have come to take possession, of the songs, the psalms, the
                                                    lamentations,

Ruth and Boaz, Jonah,
Daniel in the den of lions – for these are my stories, too,
the prophet Moshe stretching out his hand
over the sea, Yermiyahu's grief before the golden throne

of Babylon, with Markos, Mattityahu, Loukas, Yohanan...

for here is the gate of Heaven, folded open,
where we thrust our words towards the invisible, waiting for those
inaudible answers, where we thrust our prayers
into the crevices in the wall,

and speak aloud, look, here I am, oh Elohim, oh Yeshua, here I am :

The Oil-Press

Night over Yerushalayim; high, distant windows are specks
of light; the streets are dimly lit, few cars; our coach goes softly by

as if we might disturb... Even the friars of Gat-Shmanim are sleeping,
and the ancient olive trees in the garden are shapes out of prehistory.

Something sad, the shadow of a fox, perhaps, steals through the
darkness;
within us, a growing tenderness, to stay awake and watch an hour by
the rock

of agony, the Godhead stooping low, Yeshua of blood and flesh
humiliated,
hidden in the crevices of our history. There is a strained silence, for
here the Word,

uttered, is yet unutterable; I imagine fear, the dread of a great slab
of stone
lowered down onto his back, how sweat, in the chill of the night air,

dribbles down, like blood; but my own cares intervene, and when I
close my eyes
I see only the speckle-dance of my blood-cells. How can I divest myself

of self? I kneel, place hands upon the rock, but there is nothing, I
am too
comfortable in my life. I try to say I love you, to know what the
words mean...

The Word is silent, not reproachful; and can I plead with
                                        God-the-loving-
father-God-the-Breath that he ease even just a little the dreadfilled
                                                        agony

of the Lover, the name-and-nature, the wholly sensitive to the
                                                        point of
death-out-of-love? When we come out, waiting a while in the ask
                                                of moon-cold,

the deep heart-throbbing beating of the city has fallen still :

Declan

Bethlehem. The Shepherd's field… field
        of faithfulness, of David, Boaz, Ruth;
I came up out of the cave – church now, underground
        sheltering-place back then

from weathers, and from wolves – and stepped
        into a haze of sunlight, a shimmering heat,
lush hilltop, swallows in flight above high trees, a fountain,
        roses the colour of angel- and of moth-

wings, fuchsia, peach, emerald, celeste
        and I imagined them, the shepherds, ragged, scared,
their everyday lives tossed awry. And there he was,
        just standing, watching me. 'You!' I said, 'and how…?'

'No,' he said, 'not how. Ask who…'
        He smiled, and his smile was radiance
beyond the sunlight, beyond the day, though his frame
        was frail, berry-small blotches on his face,

his hands trembled, the cancer… 'No,' he said again,
        though I had not spoken. 'I have scanned the skies
for your coming, and, while you search…' He gulped, his hands
        reached a moment to his throat, 'oesophageal…

126

while you search for Yeshua, Yeshua seeks you out.' His eyes
        were clear, bright with a ravished joy.
'But you would be,' I said, 'today, your birthday,
        you would have been… 70?'

He laughed, and coughed, and gestured to the air.
        'Numbers, dates, ephemera. I am your brother,
I am your neighbour, all your neighbours, I am all
        your living, all your dead, and I am you,' he said;

'here, the shepherds built their fires, they had come back,
        quietened, suddenly shy before one another, their lives
would never be the same.' He turned away a moment, 'Feed,' he said,
        the lambs.' He was still; about us

only haze, and vapour, no birds singing, nor any breeze.
        'I gambled,' he said then, 'all I am, on love;
I opted for the Christ, for love, and care, and service; now
        the shepherds make themselves into princes,

those who should walk last have placed themselves
        in pole position; feed
the lambs.' He turned back to me: 'Speak
        everything in the light of Christ, seek out the words, the forms.'

And he was trembling, as if cold. 'You were,' I said,
        'too young, too young.' He shook his head, his smile
so radiant now it screened him in a warm glow;
        'I touched,' he said, 'the damp end wall of the cave,

I fell, hard, to the deepest place, there
        where the stillness holds, in darkness, all there is of death,
all there is of birth, and every urge of longing
        dropped away from me. I gambled all,' he said,

his voice fading, and his form. He coughed. Shuddered. 'Let me
        go now, let me be…' From somewhere came a voice
calling loudly and when I turned back there was
        sunlight only, a gentle breeze stirring amongst the roses :

The Why and Wherefore

Perhaps Yeshua, too, called out from the womb
in protest – and was not heard; nor should the woman know
what shaped itself, or who. Perhaps she stood
to watch herself shadowed on the wall, to rub, wonderingly, the taut

elliptical globe of her belly, willing
the hovering of the graces, to offer their gifts of wisdom, prophecy
and of mortality. Until her knuckles gripped
white against the rough-stone crib, sweat assaulting her skin,

her shouts were of dismay and raking pain –
how long O Elohim how long – and that wet, eyes-shut
                              too-vulnerable creature
was slapped and screaming his unwitting presence on the hard earth.

Chosen. This time, this space. Out of all other
possibilities. The why and wherefore unanswerable. A new life
swaddled in comfort. Beginning, at once, to age :

The Dead

Then Pilate asked: 'Who are you?'
The flagellation. Thorns. The cross.

On the hard floor of the praetorium
remains of the soldiers' game, the squares, the dice.

The streets. The thrusting, hostile crowds.
The shops and businesses. Pots and sieves and jars.

The souvenir shops. The ironwood crucifixes.
The city walls. The hill. The crowds.

Cloudburst in the afternoon, washing blood
down into the dust. He has to lean forward

in the struggle to find breath, dragging flesh
down against the nails. The cross,

where every border ends, and every border starts.
The earth itself, stirring in its long tremor of grief.

And all the dead strolling about the city, curious :

Gehenna, the Valley of Hinnom

Yeshua walked here, you can almost trace the footsteps,
    from the Cenacle to the Olive-Press. Perhaps the thorn moon

glistened off these tombs, Zachariah, Absolom, Bnei Hezir.
    We walk the other way, along the Kidron valley, the sun

high, demanding, the pinnacle of the temple on the right,
    a Palestinian village above us, to the left. There is someone

walking with us, and I know it's the murdered and resurrected
    Yeshua, the lover beyond compare, this the mystery, this

the God–man, this the friend. And I would touch his face, gently,
    as a blind man touches, to be acquainted. I try to listen, to silence

the noises fluent in my days, to hear that softest footfall
    moving perpetually at my side. Moshe, Shlomo, the Pentateuch,

we have come a long way from stone tablets of the law
    to the fields of grace. Swallows dive and glide above us, higher still

the waverful chalk–line of a passing jet. I would come face to face
    with the unknown companion, I have to shade my eyes in
                               the light;

there is a soft, ethereal music, Yeshua humming to himself...
    We move, slowly, along the Kidron path, talking with one
                               another

about everything that has happened. And then a boy, four years, perhaps,
   comes close, saying something, urgently, he is curly-haired, a little

ragged, and he kicks me suddenly on the knee; I want to tell him
   no, not me, I am not come to steal from you, I want to tell him

Yeshua, to speak the name aloud, here, in the valley, but the words,
   I do not have the words. There is, always to be asked, the one

question; and always to be given, the one answer. At the village edge
   old, half-beaten cars come bucket-jarring down the hill

from Friday prayer at the temple mount; fig-trees are drooping under
                                                                dust,
      long-ribbed cats, marmalade, calico and buff, stalk silently

the cheeping sparrows and one another, the world filled full
   with an insatiable hunger, a suppressed violence: and I pray

         Christ with me, the centre Christ, Christ the judge, the pardoner,
         Christ the human, the lover Christ, Christ the murdered,
                                                            the alive,

         Yeshua man, God Yeshua, Yeshua child, Yeshua ever,
         Yeshua of ages, Yeshua now, Yeshua known, misunderstood,

         Christ of revolution, of the people Christ, Christ of art and poetry,
         Christ the Crucified, the risen Christ, Christ encountered,
                                                      Christ the lost...

Above us, in the village, a child was holding a balloon, golden and high
   as the Dome of the Rock, there was a long white string, and
                                                            when –

distracted a moment by a barking dog – he let it loose, it lifted
   away from him, floating off, and he cried, calling out after it,

his young heart shattering. And then we were making the steep climb
   back to the city, the Zion Gate, and entering the restaurant,

130

the upper courtyard where we sat, at last, under parasols,
with beer, and wine, with olives, lamb and breads; I knew again

where two or three, where ten or twelve are gathered… for now
the void that is Yeshua fills me full, bone

of my bones, breaker of bread, lost and found
companion on the way; and though I heard the words:
a little while

*and you will see me no longer, and again a little while
and you will see me* – I know enough

has been given, enough given, and more than enough.